D0553529

JOB
DISCRIMINATION

how to fight...
...how to win

Jeffrey M. Bernbach

Crown Trade Paperbacks / New York

Published by Crown Trade Paperbacks, 201 East 50th Street, New York, New York 10022. Member of the Crown Publishing Group.

Random House, Inc. New York, Toronto, London, Sydney, Auckland

CROWN TRADE PAPERBACKS and colophon are trademarks of Crown Publishers, Inc.

Printed in the United States of America
Design by Jennifer Harper

Library of Congress Cataloging-in-Publication Data
Bernbach, Jeffrey.
Job discrimination : how to fight, how to win / by Jeffrey
Bernbach
    p.   cm.
1. Discrimination in employment—Law and legislation—United
States—Popular works.   I. Title.
        KF3464.Z9B47   1996
        344.73'01133—dc20
    [347.3041133]   95-34493
                CIP
        ISBN 0-517-88466-6 (pbk)
        10 9 8 7 6 5 4 3 2 1
        First Edition

For Karen—who is always there for me,

and for Moe—he would have been proud.

ACKNOWLEDGMENT

Special thanks to Rae Lindsay for her help in putting this book together. Rae, an accomplished author in her own right (17 nonfiction books), provided valuable insight and guidance as to what it takes to write a book of this type. I first knew Rae as a client, then as a contributor to *Job Discrimination: How to Fight, How to Win,* and now as a friend.

CONTENTS

AUTHOR'S NOTE

In writing *Job Discrimination: How to Fight, How to Win*, the author did not intend to offer, nor is the book to be regarded as offering, legal advice to readers. Legal advice must come from the reader's own lawyer, or through federal, state, and local antidiscrimination agencies. *Job Discrimination: How to Fight, How to Win* is intended only to provide readers with an overview of employee rights and the laws that exist to protect them. It is meant to be informative, to raise your consciousness and awareness so that you can better understand these laws and the means through which you can consider enforcing your rights. Although federal laws apply to most American workers, state laws vary widely, as do the particular facts of any individual claim. Therefore, persons who, after reading *Job Discrimination: How to Fight, How to Win*, believe they may have a valid employment discrimination claim should contact an attorney of their choice or one of the federal, state, or local anti–employment discrimination agencies.

PREFACE

For much of my legal career—including a five-year stint as a Wall Street lawyer—my area of specialization and expertise has been labor law. Historically this meant negotiating with unions, handling unfair labor practices before the National Labor Relations Board, dealing with union-organizing campaigns and elections, and being involved in grievance procedures that conclude in arbitration. Today, more and more, being a labor lawyer means handling employment discrimination cases.

After four years as chief labor counsel for The Hearst Corporation, I launched my own practice representing Hearst and other major corporations in labor disputes. In other words: I was on "their" side of the fence.

Half a century ago, employment discrimination manifested itself mainly in terms of racial, religious, ethnic, or sexual offenses, and few laws protected workers from such discrimination. But in 1964, the rights of employees were more clearly delineated when the federal government passed Title VII of the Civil Rights Act, safeguarding working men and women from all the traditional forms of discrimination except age and disability discrimination. The age gap was remedied in 1967 by the Age Discrimination in Employment Act, and disability came under the protection of federal law a few years later under the Rehabilitation Act of 1973 and again in 1991 by virtue of the Americans with Disabilities Act.

With passage of these laws, individuals began increasingly to seek legal redress from employment discrimination—initially for race discrimination, which made up the preponderance of claims for two decades—followed by age, sex, and disability discrimination cases, which burgeoned from 1984 until now and currently lead the way in employment grievances.

During all the years I defended corporations, people often asked me to represent and prosecute individuals' cases, but I refused—adhering to the bromide that you can't serve two masters. But by 1990, the demand for individual legal representation had multiplied as men and women became more aware of their rights in the workplace. (Or, perhaps this increase in litigation reflected exponentially the increase in employers' discriminatory practices against employees.)

That year, a friend asked me to do *his* friend a favor—and I did. My new client, John, was a security specialist (store detective) for a national supermarket chain. His job sounded grander than it was: Basically, he had to make sure employees and customers didn't play penny-wise games at the cash register, or eat an apple or a banana from the shelves (in supermarket parlance this is called "grazing"—far different from the yuppies' version). Both forms of theft were grounds for being fired by the vigilant supermarket chain.

John, who was around sixty-four but looked younger, applied for a promotion, and his boss turned him down: "You're too old—in six years you'll be seventy, and you'll be too old to replace me." John wasn't happy with this dead-end conclusion to his career and voiced his discontent. Dismayed at John's protest, the supermarket chain sought a way to discharge him. It hired a private investigator to follow him as he moved from store to store in an attempt to show that John's performance was poor. Eventually, based on faulty evidence, the supermarket fired him.

Our case, claiming that John had been unlawfully denied promotion because of his age and unlawfully fired in retaliation for complaining about it, hinged on the fact that John had a *good* performance record for years, and it was only *after* he complained about the no-promotion decision that the company looked for some basis to fire him. When his record was presented to the jury, and I was able to show that the company set him up through false charges of shoddy performance because it wanted to dump him, the jury decided in John's favor and awarded him double back—lost—pay (he had been earning about $35,000 a year), emotional distress damages, legal fees, and most important to John, reinstatement to his job, *plus* the promotion.

This case opened the floodgates. Two weeks later, five security specialists who had worked as a unit for a home products do-it-yourself chain and had been replaced by a younger staff heard about John's case and came to see me. The age discrimination situation here was really blatant—replacing seasoned, professional retired police officers whose ages ranged from the early fifties to the early sixties with totally inexperienced persons in their twenties. The company first defended its actions by claiming that my clients' performances were subpar. When it recognized that the evidence did not support this claim, the company alleged it had replaced my clients because as retired police officers, they could (and did) carry firearms on the job. But the company was unable to explain why this only became objectionable at the time of discharge, since my clients had carried their weapons throughout their employment at the company. Ultimately, when the company ran out of excuses, we settled favorably for my clients.

Looking back to 1990, I think several factors were at play leading to my representation of individual employees. There was a greater need for lawyers to represent individuals in employment discrimination cases—since then I've handled age, sex, disability, national origin, religion, and racial discrimination cases—and it was time for me to reexamine where I was going with my own career interests. In fact, it was time for me to move to the other side of the fence.

When it comes to employment discrimination cases, corporations largely have unlimited staff, unlimited money, and the not-so-limited ability to run roughshod over workers with less power, clout, and resources (the "deep pockets" we talk about in chapter 9). Faced with what might seem like employer invincibility, many employees who were unlawfully fired, or denied promotions, or were sexually harassed, or denied a job in the first place, would give up against these seemingly unbeatable odds.

I felt I had something to offer these individuals—not the least of which was I knew "the nature of the beast." I was uniquely qualified to understand how the corporate entities and their squads of lawyers operate. Though I continue to number corporations among my clients, individuals now comprise a great majority of my practice. Switching sides was a challenge, but well worth it. As we proceed through this last decade of the twentieth century, employment discrimination claims are escalating. Men and women who have been wrongfully discharged by "downsizing" or "rightsizing," or even—today, *thirty years after the passage of Title VII*—because they are the wrong race, or wrong size, or wrong sex, or wrong age, or have the wrong physical characteristics, deserve a fair hearing.

I don't see myself as a latter-day Atticus Finch from *To Kill a Mockingbird*. But I do see a responsibility to help those who have been discriminated against in the workplace get their day in court.

Introduction

It would not be difficult to find at least five headlines a week—or read or hear about half a dozen different cases of employment discrimination in the papers, magazines, or TV . . . in the news, business, or feature coverage. Job-related bias, unfortunately, is big news . . . and big business. On an immediate level, you or your neighbor may be a victim of on-the-job "prejudice"; on a larger level, we are aware of others who are suing to get back their jobs, or realize some compensatory rewards for being unlawfully dismissed, refused employment, or denied a promotion. On a national level, we read about sexual harassment cases, or people who have lost their jobs because they are the wrong sex, age, color, or race, or wrong physically.

Many cases make startling and intriguing headlines. For example, the secretary who sued the world's largest law firm for sexual harassment and was awarded $7.1 million; the former helicopter pilot who blew the whistle on Tailhook and received an undisclosed settlement from the navy and was awarded $6.7 million in her suit against the hotel chain for failing to protect her from sexual harassment during the now notorious convention; and the salesman who was awarded $8.4 million after suing his employer for age discrimination. Or, the woman who sued her company because she was fired for being too fat . . . and won $100,000 in lost wages and compensation . . . and won her job back.

Cases like these (and others that don't garner explosive headlines) have intrinsic merit and deserve to be heard— and won. Others, however, lack legitimate bases and represent "wishful thinking," to be charitable, or may simply be cashing in on what seems to be a "boutique" way to get legally rich overnight. The Paula Jones suit against President Clinton has resulted in thousands of inches of print publicity and dozens of hours of broadcast time, and will not be resolved for years until President Clinton is out of office.

Whatever the legal grounds behind such cases, there is no denying that as we approach the end of the twentieth century, job discrimination claims are burgeoning, and society and the legal system, employees and employers alike, will have to confront the issues, the legalities, and the possibilities of major settlements.

Since the late 1980s, there has been a veritable explosion of job discrimination cases, which have inundated federal and state antidiscrimination agencies, as well as the courts. Nationwide, since 1990, the Equal Employment Opportunity Commission (EEOC) has experienced a 37 percent increase in bias cases, from 110,000 in 1990 to 150,000 in 1993; the number of complaints rose by 60 percent in the last two years. As of October 1992, the New York office of the EEOC had a 42 percent increase over previous years, with 15,500 discrimination charges pending.

State agencies are also overwhelmed. The New York State Division of Human Rights has a backlog of 16,800 cases, many of which are over five years old, and receives about 6,000 new claims a year. The Massachusetts Commission Against Discrimination received more than 3,500 complaints last year—double the number filed in 1990. This year they expect complaints to surpass 4,200. The Pennsylvania Human Relations Commission reported 5,504 cases in 1993, more than double the 2,034 complaints of 1978.

As recently as thirty years ago, when the Beatles were claiming "All You Need Is Love" and the place to go was "Alice's Restaurant," employment discrimination largely meant *racial discrimination*.

When Title VII of the Civil Rights Act was passed in 1964, it protected employees from general on-the-job discrimination based on race, religion, sex, and national origin, but for the next two decades, the focus was mainly on racial problems. Although there is no law against harboring a prejudice, the law prohibits *acting* on that prejudice. Most of the early cases involved blacks; later on Hispanics and other minorities also brought successful suits, some of which went all the way to the Supreme Court. These suits changed the course of hiring, firing, and promoting based on race, religion, sex, or national origin. By 1984, just twenty years after Title VII, most employers were sensitized to the race issue and well aware of the power of affirmative action, discussed at length in chapter 5. Officially, *overt* racial or religious discrimination had ended.

In 1995, affirmative action (the practice, fostered by the federal government, of providing preferential treatment and/or opportunities to specified groups of persons in hiring or promotion, etc., as a means of correcting the present effects of past discrimination) began getting a good deal of negative attention. "Reverse discrimination" (the almost inevitable effect of affirmative action on those groups not benefiting from it) favoring minorities over whites, for certain positions in certain industries, has become a major issue in state courts (most notably California and Pennsylvania) and the Supreme Court. House Speaker Newt Gingrich's agenda for his Contract with America targeted affirmative action laws, and affirmative action became an important political football in the 1996 presidential campaign. Front-runner Senator Robert Dole called for a report on nationwide practices, and even President Clinton took another look at what may be discriminatory to nonminority workers. Here's the question: Is the Constitution really "color-blind," or have we swung too far in one direction? Regardless of the answer, and despite these challenges to affirmative action, a significant percentage of employment discrimination suits still involve ethnic or racial claims.

Will You Still Love Me When I'm 64? Try 50

Today, however, the major focus of employment discrimination cases has shifted to those based on *age*. Although the Age Discrimination in Employment Act of 1967 (ADEA) protects workers forty and over from being fired or denied jobs or promotions because of age, this issue remained largely quiescent for almost twenty years, like a volcano waiting to erupt. During those decades, workers in their sixties—and there were far fewer of them *then*, than there are *now* or will be *ten years from now*—were often inclined to take advantage of the "recommended retirement age" of sixty-five. Life for "senior citizens" (a term coined about fifteen years ago) was kinder, gentler: Their mortgages were either very low, or paid off, and it was possible to live somewhat comfortably on Social Security and pensions.

Age discrimination wasn't really an issue until the recession of the late 1980s, when, in a practice known as "downsizing," or more euphemistically, "rightsizing," employers looked for ways to cut expenses—these included the higher salaries and fringe benefits of older workers. All you have to do is look at some recent figures to measure the extent of "downsizing" on major American industries.

A study by *Workplace America,* a national publication focusing on job issues and trends, states that during January, February, and March of 1994 there were 135,000 layoffs, *an average of more than 2,000 for every workday.* According to Christopher W. Hunt, editor in chief of *Workplace America,* "Large companies will continue to eliminate layers and layers of management that traditionally have been in place, but which, in fact, they don't need." And those employees at the management level are more likely to be older, higher paid, and closer to gaining long-term "vested" benefits. Here are some of the major job cuts according to the *Workplace* study:

◆ **Telecommunications.** Layoffs in this industry accounted for 68,300 at six major companies in the first quarter of 1994—a figure that represents *half* of all reported layoffs. (In 1994, for example, AT&T cut 16,500 from its staff of 317,000.)

◆ **Financial Services.** Six companies were studied by

Workplace America; their total layoffs in three months amounted to 8,430, of which 5,550 (out of a total of 25,000 employees) were laid off by Fleet Financial Corporation.

◆ **Consumer Products.** The Gilette Company and Bristol-Myers Squibb between them fired 7,000 workers during that period.

◆ **Electronics.** At five companies studied, 5,200 jobs were lost—Westinghouse, which had 113,664 employees, terminated 3,400 in the first quarter of 1994.

We have not included those fired by IBM, General Motors, General Electric . . . and we all know men and women whose terminations from smaller companies didn't make headlines. When a company downsizes, that action affects *all levels* of employment, from those wearing blue collars to those wearing navy blue pinstriped suits, from assembly line, to supervisory staff, to lower-and-middle management, and right up to the top.

Late in 1995, a drastic blow to workers of all levels occurred when two of the nation's major banks, Chemical Banking Corporation and the Chase Manhattan Corporation, announced plans to merge and create the nation's largest bank. Most stockholders were thrilled, a reaction not shared by the 12,000 employees whose jobs would be eliminated because of the merger.

By the mid-1980s, after President Reagan broke the air traffic controllers' strike, those at the bottom could no longer depend on their unions to help them. Unions could no longer play the part of "Big Daddy," and the 13 or 14 percent of the workforce that had formerly relied upon their unions to fight for them were now mainly on their own. For middle-aged middle managers or supervisors, who were downsized with severance packages or "early retirement" plums that were not so sweet in the long run, not only were they *not* able to retire . . . but they also soon found out that they might not be hired for new jobs at similar stipends. For upper management, sometimes the "golden parachutes" offered for early retirement were gilded enough for execs to take the jump, and neither look back nor fight back.

What employers did not realize, however, is that today's fifty-somethings, or even forty-somethings, are a breed apart from the generation before them. Contemporary fifty-five-year-olds, influenced by society's emphasis on looking younger longer and staying fit, view themselves as being in the prime of their careers and still moving up the corporate or bureaucratic ladder. They anticipate many more years of productive employment, which for those who have started families later in life and still face paying hefty mortgages, college tuition, and other costs is financially essential. A study conducted by the National Institute on Aging and the University of Michigan shows that 40 percent of workers fifty-one through sixty-one have earned no pensions for retirement other than Social Security. Working past fifty or fifty-five therefore is often not a choice but a *necessity*. (In that vein, according to *Modern Maturity*'s survey, half of Americans fifty through sixty-four would prefer to continue working past "retirement" age.)

However, when the employment rug is rudely pulled from under them, older men and women are confronted with a drastically reduced job market and an increased likelihood of extended unemployment, which may end only with the acceptance of a lower-paying and less-satisfying job than the one they lost . . . or no job at all.

Some victims of downsizing were initially optimistic; others at all levels were scared—scared about employer retaliation if they challenged their dismissal and, remembering their parents' stories about the Depression, scared about what was ahead. Thousands—probably hundreds of thousands—didn't realize they had any legal recourse, which is one reason I decided to write this book. The fifty-five-year-old's complaint "Hey, why me—why not that thirty-five-year-old kid?" was lost in the wind.

Until many of those who had been sacked, terminated, discharged, dismissed, *fired,* and were now presented with such dire prospects and had their financial and emotional backs to the wall began to seek legal relief for their problems.

And as the seventy-six million baby boomers approach the big 5-0, and companies continue to build "profits" through downsizing, or to cut expenses by replacing older workers with "less expensive" younger employees, the issue of employment discrimination based on age will almost certainly become worse.

What's Sex Got to Do with It? Plenty

Ranking second behind age discrimination in numbers of cases filed are *sex discrimination* and *sexual harassment complaints.* While sex discrimination (denial of employment opportunities or benefits based upon gender) and sexual harassment (misconduct, based on sex) have always been a bitter fact of life for women in the workplace, until recent years only a relative few were willing to take on employers in the legal arena.

Certainly the women's rights movement encouraged such

actions. Women wanted their fair share of the market pie. But despite much public attention and many successful suits, that "glass ceiling," limiting promotional opportunities, still plagues executives who happen to be women, and women at all levels of employment still make only seventy cents for every dollar earned by men in the same position.

Some strides have been made in the rights of pregnant women. The Pregnancy Discrimination Act of 1978, an amendment to Title VII, prohibits discrimination on the basis of pregnancy or, in fact, maternity. (Maternity leave, however, varies by state, company size, etc.)

While the uphill battle for sexual equality continues to be fought at what may seem like a snail's pace of victories, *sexual harassment,* which has always been a problem and which many women "just dealt with," came to national (probably worldwide) attention with the Anita Hill–Clarence Thomas controversy in 1991. (It should be noted that until 1989, Thomas chaired the Equal Employment Opportunity Commission—EEOC.) The much-televised, much-publicized case went to the very hearts of women, who are now filing sexual harassment claims in record numbers. This is not to suggest that women do not continue to experience the same fears and trepidation regarding retaliation by employers, and possible damage to their future careers as a result of speaking out and challenging discriminatory employment practices. They absolutely do, but they are now willing to risk the consequences of fighting to vindicate their legal rights.

Aided by the passage of the Civil Rights Act of 1991, with its wider remedial provisions, and the broad definition of sexual harassment being adopted by the courts, women who feel they have been discriminated against because of their sex, or have been sexually harassed, are asserting themselves as never before.

Ready, Willing, Able to Work: Capable or Disabled?

Although age and sex lead the field, moving quickly toward third place on the most active list of job-related abuses are complaints of *disability discrimination*. Prohibited by various states for many years, and for federal contractors (by the Rehabilitation Act of 1973), discrimination based on disability became unlawful *nationwide* with the passage of the Americans with Disabilities Act of 1991 (ADA), which covers physical problems far beyond "traditional" disabilities. Under the ADA, an employee cannot be discriminated against because he or she has AIDS, or is too fat, or may lack the "right" image for the job. The courts and antidiscrimination agencies are still struggling with the definition of *disability* and *handicap* in the context of employment discrimination, but there is every indication that the result will be a very broad definition, which will facilitate and encourage employees to file suit.

New Dimensions in Race, Religious, Ethnic Bias

Thirty years after the passage of Title VII, employers are sensitized to traditional discrimination, most of which was aimed first at African-Americans and later at Hispanic-Americans. But such bias actions are still prevalent, though often with a different twist, or aimed at a different group.

Asians, for example, are a current target. Other immigrants—chiefly illegal aliens—are the focus of job bias, especially in California (which passed the much disputed Proposition 187 in the November 1994 election), and in New York, New Jersey, Texas, Illinois, Arizona, and Florida, where state budgets and the local economy are burdened by the need to provide services for "newcomers."

At some times, though, as with other forms of job bias, complaints of racism may be "convenient" or even opportunistic. Clarence Thomas, for example, a former chief executive of the EEOC, fell back on charges of "electronic lynching" during the Supreme Court confirmation hearings at which Anita Hill leveled accusations of sexual harassment at him. Another individual recently in the news, who was investigated for a $350 million-dollar trading scam at a major investment banking firm, had reportedly always been vehemently *against* affirmative action. Yet while fighting the charges against him, he is said to have claimed he had been unfairly treated because of racism, despite his employer's belief that it had strong reasons to be concerned by his alleged financial maneuverings and misdealings.

As I indicated earlier, the major reason I decided to write this book stems from the sure knowledge that there are hundreds of thousands of victims of employment discrimination—in all its nasty guises—who have not, or will not, challenge their termination, or denial of a promotion or other mistreatment by a current employer, or the inability to get a better job, *because they don't realize they are protected from such actions by federal and state laws* ... or because they are frightened to fight the "big guys" ... or because they feel they don't have the financial resources to engage in such a battle.

Job Discrimination: How to Fight, How to Win lays out the parameters for combating the various forms of employment discrimination, with guidelines ranging from how to tell if you have a viable discrimination claim, all the way to waging your fight in court. I've included case histories of clients I've represented, as well as breakthrough suits that have made national headlines.

Aside from my major goal of providing an awareness of applicable laws and step-by-step information for pursuing a discrimination claim, I also hope to help restore an element that goes far beyond financial consideration. When a person loses a job, is denied a promotion, is sexually harassed, or is relegated to a lesser post because of age, sex, race, religion, or ethnicity, or a physical handicap or illness, the emotional consequences often far exceed any financial losses.

The greater loss is that of self-esteem. The feeling that "I can't take care of myself" or "I can't provide for my family" is drastic, devastating. What we lawyers describe as "emotional distress" must never be taken lightly. I hope that what follows in *Job Discrimination: How to Fight, How to Win* not only provides a plan of action, but also shores up and reestablishes the sense of self-worth and pride that is so badly battered when one is a victim of employment discrimination.

◆   ◆   ◆

PART ONE

Employment Discrimination
and How to
Recognize It

You *know* you have done a good job . . . but somehow, you weren't promoted or given a raise, or worse, you've been fired. Maybe you were too old or too pregnant, or a member of the "wrong" sex, religion, race, or ethnic group, or disabled by illness or a physical characteristic. Maybe your boss or another co-worker sexually harassed you and made your life miserable. If any of these (and other) descriptions apply as reasons why you suffered workplace discrimination, you may be in what is known as a "protected category," and as such, you have a federally mandated right to seek justice in the form of getting your job back, receiving that promotion, plus compensatory, punitive, or other (financial) satisfaction for what's happened to you.

What identifies you as "protected"? The definitions are established in Title VII of the Civil Rights Act of 1964 (usually referred to as Title VII), which prohibits discrimination in employment based on race, color, religion, national origin, or sex; the Age Discrimination in Employment Act of 1967 (ADEA), which prohibits discrimination on the basis of age; and the Americans with Disabilities Act of 1991 (ADA), which prohibits discrimination based on an employee's disability.

However, being in a protected category is not all it takes to determine whether you have a prima facie (basic) claim of employment discrimination. To proceed successfully under Title VII, the ADEA, or the ADA, you must be able to answer four questions in the affirmative:

1. *Are you in a "protected class"?* In other words, are you a minority, or over age forty, or suffering a disability, or was your sex, religion, or national origin the issue?

2. *Were you qualified for the position in question—* either to be hired for this job, or for a promotion, or not to have been fired from your job?

3. *Did you suffer an adverse employment decision—*such as not being hired or promoted, or were you fired?

4. *Did the situation occur under circumstances that could be interpreted as a discriminatory action?* For example, was the company's "reason" for doing what it did untrue and was the job in question given to someone substantially younger, or of a different sex, race, or religion, or someone who lacked your particular physical disability?

Bluntly stated, if you can't meet these four tests, if you can't answer yes to all four of these questions, you're not in the ball game regarding an employment discrimination claim. But one can readily see the answers to these questions are not always "black and white." The answers to questions one and three are generally pretty clear and not subject to dispute. On the other hand, the answers to questions two and four, involving as they do issues of motive, intent, and judgment, are frequently in the "gray" area and therefore comprise the battleground for most employment discrimination lawsuits.

Whatever form of employment discrimination you feel has victimized you, the legal process to be followed in redressing your grievance is largely the same. The first step is to file a complaint within the time allowed (sometimes 180 days, sometimes 300 days after the discriminatory act) with the *federal agency* (the EEOC), or with a *state civil rights agency* that protects employee rights, such as the New York Division of Human Rights. (Most states have similar agencies, and they are usually listed in the State Government section under the Labor Department or the Department of Human Rights in your telephone book.) You then have the option of allowing the agency to seek a resolution of your claim or moving on to a lawsuit in federal or state court. (Specific details about these procedures are discussed in chapter 6.)

The EEOC, as well as state human rights agencies, were established to address employment discrimination problems in the expectation that they would assist in settling or resolving them and thereby prevent clogging up federal and state courts with discrimination cases. Therefore, in theory, employees are required to file with the appropriate agency *first* to give this agency a chance to do its job. What has happened though, as I noted earlier, is that the state agencies and the EEOC are so overburdened that they can't get to most cases for two, three, or more years . . . and the waiting game is increasing as people become more and more aware of their rights and are filing a record number of employment discrimination complaints.

Getting back to whether or not you have a *viable* claim, let's say you can establish the four elements of the prima facie case we talked about. The employer, by way of defense, is then permitted to offer a legitimate, nondiscriminatory reason for the actions it took. Then the burden of proof is on *you*, the *plaintiff*, to prove your case by a preponderence of the evidence; that is, to show that your claims against your former, or would-be, employer are *more likely true than not true.*

This is different from criminal cases, where the prosecutor must prove *beyond a reasonable doubt* that the defendant is *guilty*. For example, in the media-saturated O. J. Simpson case, the burden of proof rested in the prosecution's hands—they had to prove beyond a "reasonable doubt" that O. J. was guilty of murdering his wife and her friend. In employment discrimination cases, which are "civil cases," what you as plaintiff have to establish for the judge and jury is that your side of the story is *more believable* than what your employer is proposing. In other words, the scale of justice tips slightly more in your favor.

But you must be able to support your claim. Can you convince an agency, or, if you take your case to court, a judge and jury, that you were discriminated against in your workplace? Can you provide documentation, dates, or witnesses who will back up your story? Remember that whether or not you choose to present your case through a state agency or the EEOC, or with the help of an attorney, via the state or federal court system, you must be able to provide evidence (testimony, documents, or other information) to support your charges. In subsequent chapters we will talk about this, as well as the ammunition your employer and its attorneys will likely use.

Okay, you establish the four prima facie case points, you have documentation and testimony, you file your claim with the EEOC or a state agency, *or,* you decide to have an attorney represent you in either state or federal court. What can you gain from such action if you win? Here are the types of "redress"—as we lawyers term the ways in which wrongs are righted—available to victims of discrimination, and of course they vary, as we will discuss in subsequent chapters:

◆ **Back (lost) pay.** Salary and benefits you would have earned from the time you were denied a job, or promotion, or were fired, until the time your case goes to trial. In age discrimination cases, this amount is usually doubled if it can be shown that the employer acted willfully (engaged in the discriminatory act with knowledge that it was unlawful or with reckless disregard to its lawfulness). This doubling is called "liquidated damages."

◆ **Front (future) pay.** Your earnings after trial had you stayed on the job for a certain amount of time (for example, ten years, or until you retired) may be granted at the judge's, or sometimes the jury's, discretion.

or

◆ **Reinstatement.** Getting back the job (or promotion) you were denied may also be granted at the judge's discretion.

◆ **Punitive damages.** This is a monetary award (available under Title VII or the ADA) against your employer or ex-employer, to punish it for having committed a serious wrong and to act as a deterrent to similar conduct in the future. Employee attorneys like to argue that for punitive damages to fulfill their purpose, the larger the employer, the greater the amount of punitive damages that should be awarded.

◆ **Compensatory damages (emotional distress).** Was your health and emotional well-being adversely affected? Was there pain and suffering because you couldn't take care of your family? Did you lose sleep because you were in jeopardy of losing your home? Monetary awards to compensate you for going through such emotional turmoil come under the broad umbrella called "compensatory damages." The amount of damages generally is decided by a jury if the case goes to trial. If you elect to proceed before a judge without a jury (which although unusual does sometimes happen) or your case is processed through an antidiscrimination agency (which does not employ a jury), compensatory damages will be determined by the judge.

◆ **Legal fees.** If your case is tried, and you win, the losing employer may be obligated to pay any legal fees you have incurred. If the case is settled out of court, usually you will be responsible for your attorney's fees.

While these forms of redress are certainly comprehensive and tempting, I'd like to offer two caveats. First, you have to understand going in that neither you, the victim, nor your lawyer can ever know for sure whether you will be able to *prove* your claim to a judge or jury. As a lawyer, if I take on your case, it means I believe in it, I "know" it, I can feel it, but can I always prove it? If you're looking for some kind of guarantee, I must say at the outset, there's no such thing. The only one who knows *absolutely* if you're a victim of discrimination is the *person who discriminated against you*—only he (or they) know the real motivation for the firing or denial of promotion or failure to hire you—and they are not likely to admit it. You must prove your case through other approaches, which are discussed later on.

The second caveat is to measure the widespread publicity about employment discrimination cases very carefully. On the one hand, all the headlines serve a good purpose— they focus attention on workplace bias and make people more aware of their rights. The downside of this, however, is that employees see the headlines and envision multimillion-dollar payoffs. More often than not, this is wishful thinking. Understand right now, that if after reading this book and considering all the variables and uncertainties in employment discrimination cases, you feel you have a legitimate case, then go for it. However, keep the multimillion-dollar settlements or awards in perspective (like winning the lottery), and place your attention on what you have a legitimate right to fight for and a realistic expectation of what you will gain if you win.

Chapter 1

Fifty and Fired:
Age Discrimination

Not long ago, George Foreman (just two months short of his forty-sixth birthday) put on a pair of twenty-year-old velvet trunks and a very positive attitude, and climbed into a boxing ring where, after ten rounds, he knocked out Michael Moorer (age twenty-six) to regain the heavyweight championship he had lost to Muhammad Ali twenty years earlier.

But Foreman almost lost his fight before he fought it. Moorer's promoters wanted a match against a younger man. It was necessary for Foreman to file an age discrimination suit in the state of Nevada before the World Boxing Association "bowed to the law and the rights of the aged," as the *New York Times* phrased it, and approved the match.

Boxers are considered "elderly" at forty; so are rock stars like Mick Jagger and Paul McCartney (both grandfathers, both over fifty), and models like Lauren Hutton (also fifty-plus). Best-selling author and early proponent of feminism Betty Friedan, who recently published *The Fountain of Age,* saw Foreman's Battle of the Ages fight as a metaphor for such age breakthroughs. "It's simply a myth that these great accomplishments don't happen to many people after a certain age," she told the *Times.* "And you know who is going to break through that mystique, that myth? The baby boomers . . . all heading for their fiftieth birthdays."

With all due respect to Friedan, Jagger, McCartney, Hutton, et al., *exceptions* don't prove the rule. In fact, as we head swiftly toward the millennium, the 2.7 million Americans who turned fifty in 1993 and the seventy-six million baby boomers who are right behind them, plus those workers ten or fifteen years older, are experiencing the biggest wave of employment discrimination since the Age Discrimination in Employment Act of 1967 (ADEA) made it illegal to fire anyone over forty, or deny them hiring or promotions, *because of their age.* According to EEOC statistics, 31,146 charges of age discrimination were filed in 1993, a 173 percent increase over the 11,397 cases filed in 1980. And these do not include cases filed with state agencies.

There's a terrible irony here. Workers over forty don't think of themselves as senior citizens, or even "junior" senior citizens, because of the pervasive emphasis on youth, staying fit, looking younger longer, etc. But when their employers decide to "downsize to cut costs," the old rule of "last in (hired), first out (fired)" has now become a case of eliminating the highest paid workers (read that, "older workers"), where obviously you save the most money. Or, here's another irony: Employers may feel that workers over forty don't present the "right" image, no matter how slim and trim they are.

The "image" syndrome was all too apparent to me a few years ago when Barbara, a very attractive, energetic woman in her early forties, came to my office regarding what she felt was an unfair dismissal. Barbara, who now works out three or four times a week and rides a horse in Central Park, formerly put in fourteen-hour days as an advertising executive. In March 1989, she left a good position to take a better one at a trade magazine. She called it her "dream job. The salary was right. Everything." That dream job lasted just six months until she was fired in August, replaced by two younger women. After suing her former employer for age discrimination in June 1990, we settled the case in November 1992. (When a suit is settled, as opposed to tried in court, the settlement agreement usually provides, as did Barbara's, that its terms must be kept confidential.)

How did we persuade Barbara's former employer to settle? The usual way. During the progress of the lawsuit, we developed evidence showing that the so-called reason for firing Barbara (falsifying her expense account) was in itself false and nothing more than a convenient excuse to fire her because of her age. The employer, or at least its attorneys, recognized that juries can be "funny" about these things. When they "smell a rat," they are often inclined to remedy the mischief. Rather than take its chances with the jury, the employer wisely opted for settlement.

But here's a case of a vibrant, enthusiastic, and clearly professional woman who was put out to pasture, as they say. It took courage and guts for her to file that suit. She knew in a sense she would be a "marked woman" in her field. As she said in interviews afterward, "A suit is not for the lighthearted. It's an intense emotional roller coaster. Once you sue your employer, you're marked as a person who sues. And if I lost, I'd be marked a loser. So I took this fifteen-year career and put it on the line, and we went through this roller coaster for almost three years." Barbara didn't return to her former profession; today she runs a travel business and is able to enjoy more free time than she ever had before.

Although Barbara's "image" was quite youthful, it wasn't youthful enough to prevent her firing. And, of course, the two younger women who replaced her probably provided a "twofer" for her company, in the sense that together they weren't as old as Barbara and collectively didn't earn much more than Barbara had on her own.

It's no secret that in certain glamour or high-powered fields—broadcast and print media, selling stocks and bonds or commodities trading, publishing and advertising, to name a few—a worker is considered burned out at about forty or forty-five.

Not long ago, I took on the case of a forty-three-year-old metals trader for a major bank who had been fired under what could only be considered bizarre circumstances. On a fateful June day in 1993, he was told by his boss that as a result of reduction in staff at the bank, his job was being eliminated effective the following September. Unless the bank could find another job for him, he would be discharged at that time. David, as we will call him, was told that he need not report to work but would be paid through September.

Although the bank made a few halfhearted attempts to place David in another position, nothing came of it, and September was fast approaching. Dave consulted me and revealed two very interesting facts: first, his job was the only one targeted for elimination in the so-called reduction of staff; and second, he had overheard his two immediate bosses discussing how they needed some *new young blood* on the metals trading desk. At that point, since Dave was still on the payroll, I decided it would be best for him to have a frank talk with the bank about what he knew, rather than plunging right into a lawsuit. Dave had this talk, and the bank kept him on the payroll but told him he still didn't have to report to work.

David tried diligently to find another job in the next few months, but his efforts met with no success. Then, in June, one full year after the last time he had actually reported to work, the bank finally terminated his employment, telling David how generous it had been to pay his salary for the entire year that he hadn't actually worked. Because "generosity" did not negate the bank's original discriminatory motivation, we sued. The bank sought to have the case dismissed because David had waited too long after he was first told he would be fired the previous June to file (exceeded the applicable statute of limitations). The court agreed with us that while David had, indeed, failed to bring his suit within the time provided, his failure to do so was the result of the bank's actions lulling him into a false sense of security. The court then denied the bank's request to throw out David's suit. Now, faced with having to try to defend its actions and statements, which reflected age discrimination, the bank settled. Dave has gotten a new job and is moving on with his life.

While Barbara and David were in their forties, most age discrimination cases involve workers over fifty. A landmark age bias case in 1994 involved a former network news correspondent who had garnered top reviews—praises and raises, as I call them—but was abruptly fired by the network. In 1991, at age fifty-four, this veteran reporter who had worked for the network for twenty-three years, heading up news coverage in Lebanon, Northern Ireland, Bangladesh, and Beijing, was told his job was being eliminated "to cut costs." In the months that followed, he told reporters he became depressed, gained weight, and considered committing suicide. Testifying on his behalf was another veteran reporter, age sixty-three, who was fired in 1993 after twenty-eight years with the network, who said that younger people in the Rome bureau (where he had been working) were transferred rather than fired. Another supportive witness was a fifty-year-old former production manager with twenty-seven years employment before she was fired in 1991, who currently has her own age discrimination suit pending.

According to published reports, the bureau chief's case was "amicably settled" for an undisclosed amount on the fourth day of trial. The former TV executive, who currently lives in Europe, had sued for back pay and damages, estimated at about $1 million.

While our focus has been on employees in their forties and fifties, we must not forget that shrinking, yet still important, group of employees in their sixties. Remember, there is no upper age limit to the ADEA's protection. Persons who are willing and able are by law entitled to work as long as they like, provided they can do their job adequately.

This brings to mind the former executive assistant to a forty-nine-year-old top executive of a textile empire. After working for his boss for about fifteen years, my client was summarily dismissed from his job—days before his sixty-fifth birthday—because, he was told, he was "uncooperative." All of a sudden, the same personality traits that had been acceptable to his boss for all those years were now objectionable. Howie sued, and the company sought to have the case dismissed. In support of its motion (written request to the court) for dismissal of our executive assistant's lawsuit, the textile company submitted affidavits (sworn statements) of numerous present and former co-workers attesting to Howie's "uncooperative" nature. Each of the co-workers related one or more anecdotes about his "offensive" behavior.

And Howie's boss himself spoke of the "final straw" being my client's causing another newly employed worker to quit his job because of Howie's high-handed manner. As it turned out, we developed evidence showing that the new employee had actually told the company that he was leaving because he found the work too arduous. We also found out that the company was interviewing a possible replacement for my client *weeks* before his discharge. Relying on these facts, as well as its perception that the complaints of lack of cooperation were "old news," the court denied the request to dismiss the case, which was settled a short time later.

Recently the *Wall Street Journal* ran an article headlined "Over the Hill," noting that "Employees, at 50, are seen as rigid, expendable." The writers pointed out that "Gray hair is expected in the executive suite but is becoming quite unfashionable in middle management and lower down in the ranks." In that article, an executive recruiter was quoted as saying, "None of my clients ever ask for someone over 50 . . . age discrimination is the workplace issue of the 1990s. Instead of a 50-year-old, employers want a 30-year-old who costs a lot less and doesn't give you any funny looks when you say 'leap over the wall.' "

But there are older workers who aren't able or willing to "leap over the wall," who still are entitled to their rights and can successfully enforce them in court. Take heart from this story about a sixty-seven-year-old, who, in July 1991, was fired "for poor performance" from his job as a salesman for a major northeastern corporation after thirty-five years with the company. Now, although I warned you about getting your hopes up over million-dollar-plus awards, in 1994 a jury awarded the salesman $435,000 in compensatory damages and $8 million in punitive damages. This veteran sales whiz had turned down early retirement in 1989 and 1990 because he "couldn't afford to retire," and by law he had every right to continue working.

As we have noted previously, the right to be free from age discrimination in the workplace was specifically enacted in 1967, which protected workers between the ages of forty and sixty-five. This was subsequently increased to age seventy, and, in 1986, the ADEA was amended to eliminate *any mandatory retirement age at all for most workers*. Today, under federal law, it is unlawful for any employer (employing twenty or more employees for at least twenty weeks per year) to discriminate against employees or job applicants who are forty or older because of their age. As with any rule, there are exceptions, limited as they may be. Certain highly paid executives and persons in major policy-making positions may still be subject to mandatory retirement at age sixty-five, and law enforcement officers, firefighters, state judges, and tenured university faculty are subject to mandatory retirement at age seventy.

Consider the irony here: The jurists and legislators who establish the laws are so often *above them,* and are under no such constraints regarding age. One of many congressional "éminences grises" who served well past traditional retirement age is South Carolina's Senator Strom Thurmond, who, by his early nineties, had served fifty-plus years in Congress and at age 92 had a reelection fund in place for his next term. And Ronald Reagan, approaching eighty when he left office, established a record as our oldest president. Federal judges and Supreme Court justices are appointed "for life." Many have stayed on well into their seventies and eighties, and they often don't retire from the bench until forced to by death or illness (for example, Thurgood Marshall, William O. Douglas, and William Brennan).

Another exception to the general rule prohibiting age from being a determining factor in employment decisions is when, and *only* when, it is a "bona fide occupational requirement" for job performance. This occurs when there is evidence to support the conclusion that advancing age might so impair the abilities of an employee to perform his or her duties that it would disqualify them or present a danger to the public safety. For example, it might be prudent (and legal) to dismiss a seventy-five-year-old woman from a job as a nursery school aide. Despite the generations of expertise she might have, the exertion of caring for toddlers all day could be beyond a septuagenarian's physical capabilities.

That's a somewhat easy call to make. But consider the commercial pilot who has flown planes since he was fourteen and, at age fifty-seven, challenged the Federal Aviation Administration's "age sixty" rule, which was established in 1959 because the FAA thought physical and mental functions deteriorated with aging and therefore would make pilots over sixty a safety hazard. The pilot said the rule represents "craziness, absolute craziness," and accurately states, "The president of the United States is routinely over sixty, to say nothing of Congress and the Senate."

The pilot told reporters "airline accidents in recent years have been attributed in many instances to pilot inexperience, not to older, more experienced pilots." So far his case, pending in the U.S. Circuit Court of Appeals, has produced no comments from the FAA, which has never granted an exception to the "age sixty" rule.

However, in another recent case, a pilot *did* prevail on his claim of age discrimination against a major airline that had fired him upon reaching age sixty. That case was also significant because of the U.S. Supreme Court's decision that back pay and liquidated (punitive) damages in age discrimination lawsuits are subject to federal income tax.

Explaining the decision, Justice John Paul Stevens wrote, "Whether one treats [an individual's] attaining the age of sixty or his being laid off on account of his age as the proximate cause of [his] loss of income, neither the birthday nor the discharge can fairly be described as a 'personal injury' or 'sickness.' " Although this mid-1995 ruling is specifically applicable to age discrimination cases, it may not bode well for the non-taxability of back pay and punitive damages recovered in other types of unemployment discrimination suits.

Should a pilot, at sixty, be considered as capable of flying a plane as George Bush, who at sixty-four was our forty-third president and was deemed capable of piloting not only the country but also his beloved "cigarette" speedboat? If a pilot shouldn't fly past sixty because he is entrusted with protecting hundreds of lives on each flight, should there be mandatory retirement for surgeons of the same age who routinely work in one-to-one "life-threatening" situations?

And what about something as seemingly benign as teaching? One age (and gender) discrimination suit by a college professor with a Ph.D. who a decade earlier had been an assistant professor in a prominent college's biology department until she was denied tenure was won in the United States District court, only to be reversed by the U.S. Court of Appeals. The evidence showed that for seven years every male biologist at the college was paid a salary greater than this fifty-three-year-old married woman, and the U.S. judge handling the case determined that between 1956 and 1986 not one married woman had received tenure in any of the six "hard" sciences (biology, chemistry, geology, mathematics, physics, and computer science).

During the course of the trial, evidence was offered showing that the assistant professor's academic, research, and teaching skills (as well as the number of classes and students she taught) were superior to those of three men and one younger, unmarried woman who had been granted the tenure she was denied. The judge awarded her full tenure with double back pay for seven years, a package that amounted to about $1 million.

However, in late 1995, a three-judge panel of the Court of Appeals dismissed the assistant professor's case, ruling that the statistics relied upon by the District Court were "gerrymandered." The Court of Appeals also said that the college had the right to take into consideration the assistant professor's eight-year hiatus from academia in order to raise her children as a factor in her tenure review, commenting that "a policy may discriminate between those employees who take off long periods of time in order to raise children and those who either do not have children or are able to raise them without an appreciable career interruption." Because this opinion appears to be contrary to the laws protecting women from discrimination based on maternity, it will in all likelihood be challenged in future litigation.

What you really have here is a simple difference of opinion by two different courts hearing the same evidence. Does it mean that the first court to consider the case was wrong, and the second one right? In the absolute sense, propably not. However, in the real world of litigation, the decision of the higher Court (the Court of Appeals) controls.

Like the ADEA, state laws also prohibit an employer from firing a worker because of his age. However, sometimes satisfying the burden of proving the wrongful motivation under state law can be more difficult. Two-thirds of the United States are "employment at will" states in which employers can fire employees arbitrarily, or "at will"—for no reason at all (unless they have written employment contracts), even if, let's say, it's because they don't like the color of the car you drive. On the other hand, making the employee's burden easier, the remaining states have "wrongful discharge" laws, essentially requiring a valid reason for discharging an employee. Currently, the National Employment Lawyers Association is lobbying for a federal bill that would protect all employees from being fired "at will."

Because the college that denied tenure to the assistant professor was located in an "employment at will" state, the college had the right under state law to fire her for *any reason except those falling into the category of employment discrimination*. In this case, the "at will" law was of no help to the college because its actions contravened federal anti-discrimination laws. The judge who heard the case concluded that the professor had a viable suit for *both* age and sex discrimination and found that the college's evaluation of the assistant professor's credentials was tainted by "bad faith," "purposeful dishonesty," "spurious criticism," "misrepresented facts," "distorted numbers," and revealed a "patently discriminatory" attitude. Thus, she prevailed under both federal and state law.

From 1985 until 1994, when the suit finally was won, the assistant professor was fortunate to gain employment, first for one year as a half-time adjunct professor, and later, after earning a master's degree in social work, as a counselor for a county mental hygiene department.

Others have not been as fortunate. In 1985, a megapharmaceuticals corporation, after losing its patent for one of the most widely prescribed tranquilizers in the world, downsized drastically, laying off 1,222 people at one of its corporate facilities. Collectively 478 of these ex-employees filed a class action age discrimination suit for as much as $100 million. One manager in the drug company's chemical production department, who has since been fired and has joined the class action suit, is candid about what happened a decade ago. "We knew we weren't supposed to discriminate based on age," he told a local newspaper in October 1994, noting that managers "looked at a lot of other" factors. Ultimately, though, age became the main factor. "If you want to cut dollars, you don't cut the new person. You look at the person who is making a lot of money, and by golly, those are the older people."

Generally, the members of this class action suit (a lawsuit brought by a number of persons on behalf of all other similarly situated workers who will share in any award resulting from the suit) averaged earnings of $50,000 a year, had been with the company over fifteen years, and were in their early fifties when they were fired. Of this group, twenty-eight have died, many of them are underemployed, earning less than they had at the pharmaceuticals company, several have been unemployed for almost a decade, and several have committed suicide. *All* of them are emotionally distressed over what happened to them.

One "class member" is a former chemist who had been with the company for thirty-five years and received the traditional gold watch just three weeks before he was terminated. Another is a computer specialist and self-described "company man" who in his eighteen years at the company had been rewarded with over half a dozen promotions and regular raises. Since he was fired, this computer executive has experienced difficulty holding a job—his confidence is shot, and he says he is "introverted and depressed." He is now on permanent disability.

Often the large number of people in class action suits can be their greatest strength but may turn out to be their greatest weakness. One of the problems with this and other class action suits is that by involving so many people the legal machinery can grind to a halt. For example, how do you get depositions (sworn pretrial testimony) from all these ex-employees, some of whom have died? At the minimum it gives the employer and its attorneys a golden opportunity to stall and delay the case. Originally, defense lawyers for the pharmaceutical company sought depositions from all 478 class members. Their request was eventually lowered to 100; the employees' attorneys would like to limit depositions to 20.

However, it should not be assumed, based on the horror stories of the assistant professor and the pharmaceuti-

cal company employees, that the only way in which employers seek to reduce the number of older employees on
their payroll is through blatantly illegal actions. A more
subtle approach occurs when, despite their years of experience and obvious usefulness to employers, fiftyish employees who are generally the most highly paid (read:
expensive for the company) near early retirement age (frequently fifty-five). They are often susceptible or receptive
to severance packages that revolve around retirement benefits, especially when they are scared, afraid not to take
what's offered, and worried about what will happen to
them if they sue. The severance packages are frequently
"sold" by employers on the basis that they are a one-time
opportunity offered in a climate in which there is no guarantee that the employee's job will exist in the future.

Softening the abrupt dismissal blow by offering early retirement packages and severance pay has proven very effective. A big chunk of money can be quite attractive to
some men and women, particularly when they are not
aware that they have been the victim of age discrimination.
A card-playing buddy of mine, for example, never mentioned to me that he had lost his $95,000 a year (plus
bonuses) job because, as he later said, he felt he could easily find another one, and the severance package was very
good. But the severance package is not free. The price is
signing a release, waiving any right to sue the company for
employment discrimination.

My friend signed the release, believing he was still "on
the ladder . . . going to be a VP at another company in a
couple of years." Three years later, he still hadn't found another job, after sending out five hundred résumés (which
netted ten interviews). After the fact, when I couldn't help

him, my friend told me that "I didn't even think of age discrimination, because I was only fifty-two, and I felt I presented a much younger image."

I don't know what it says about the friends I have, but this was not an isolated case. Another friend who was fired by the same company about a year later also accepted the severance package offered to him and signed the release with waiver of right to sue. While his expectations of finding a new job paralleled those of his colleague, his motivation for accepting the severance package and waiving his right to sue was a bit different. He had been with the company for twenty years and had advanced to a high-paying ($100,000 plus) management position. He was a company man through and through (had the company store sold boxer shorts bearing its logo, they would have been all he wore). Because of his loyalty to his employer, it did not, nor would it ever, occur to him that his beloved company might actually have discriminated against him—or, put another way, that it was the very same twenty years employment, which engendered his fierce loyalty, that ultimately, at age fifty, led to his discharge.

When I last spoke with my friend not long ago, he had begun a new career in the travel business at a fraction of his former salary and bonuses. Not only had his optimism about his future job prospects dimmed, but he also had taken a hard look at his former employer's pattern of systematically eliminating fiftyish employees from the payroll. Today, he is angry about this. Given a chance to do it over again, my friend is quick to say he would have consulted a lawyer. He tells others approaching their fiftieth year to "take off the rose-colored glasses" when their employer offers them a "package"; it may look good in the short run, but if discrimination is afoot, make sure they know the legal alternative to simply taking it with a smile and any traditional token for loyalty and longevity.

To be sure, in some cases the "golden parachutes" offered as a retirement incentive are big enough to negate any discrimination suit, regardless of the employer's intent in offering them. Recently, two men sought my advice. One had a severance package for $220,000; the other $110,000. I was very careful to point out clearly to each of them that if they passed up the offered severance packages they could lose everything. As I've said, the outcome of a lawsuit is never guaranteed. At some point legal action is not worth the risk. Let's say you're offered a $220,000 severance package, and in a successful employment discrimination lawsuit you could be awarded double or even triple that amount. Is it worth the risk involved in passing up almost a quarter of a million dollars? That would be a personal decision but one that should give great consideration to the risks of losing it all.

For any employee over forty who is suddenly, abruptly, without reason dismissed, please heed this caution. Do not accept a severance package (unless it is so great), at the price of signing a release, without talking to an attorney first. Signing a waiver eliminates any opportunity you may have to sue for age discrimination. Actually, under current law, in order to avoid a subsequent challenge to the enforceability of a release, employers will generally recommend that the employee being offered the severance package consult with an attorney prior to signing the release.

Unfortunately, many people don't really know what it's like to be out of a job at age fifty . . . until it happens to you. A current client, Jo, who turned sixty three months after she was fired, came to me almost punch-drunk. "How could they do this? They always told me how great I looked and what a good job I was doing." Instead of retreating into depression, she's become an "expert" on age discrimination and helped to prepare her own case every step of the way. This is not so different from the situation when someone becomes ill. That patient and/or their families become very knowledgeable about that illness. And in both situations, this knowledge can be quite helpful.

By the same token, learning the real facts behind one's discharge can be devastating. Jo now recognizes that hers is truly an *All About Eve* situation in which she groomed her young assistant, praised her, obtained raises and promotions for her . . . and then was stabbed in the back when two key executives of the company decided that the young, attractive, flirtatious "Eve" (who gave them a "she goes or I go" choice) could do the job as publicity director—after all, Jo had taught her everything she knew. The problem now is that Jo can't find another job.

At age sixty in today's youth-oriented job market, under the best of circumstances, the deck is stacked against Jo. Most positions she's qualified for ask for "salary history," and her salary history places her in the $50,000-plus category; if she applies for jobs that pay less, she's told she's "overqualified." If she applies for jobs that pay $50,000 or more, she has to explain why she was supposedly fired for "performance—inability to manage a department." Sure, she knows that her former assistant wanted *her* job and played upon her male superiors' preference for a twenty-eight-year-old over a sixty-year-old. But how does she give an explanation that sounds like something other than "sour grapes"? It is a story that likely will play out better in court than at a job interview. Therefore, Jo, who is not a litigious person, concluded that the best way for her to deal with what happened to her was through an age discrimination suit.

When it finally dawned on Jo's former employers that, if necessary, she was prepared to proceed all the way to trial, the case took some interesting turns. As it became increasingly apparent that the stated reason for Jo's discharge—poor performance—would not hold up, Jo's former employer became more desperate. At the deposition of its president, held some eight months into the lawsuit, the employer lamely and belatedly identified a new and previously unrevealed alleged basis for Jo's termination: a "drinking problem." The president testified that it was based on one or two chance encounters he had had with Jo on the elevator a year or two previously during which he smelled alcohol on her breath. He admitted, however, that the encounters may well have been *after* business lunches at which Jo had entertained authors or media contacts, where cocktails were customary, and that his olfactory senses could not discern whether she had had more than a single drink during each lunch. He also conceded that he had neither spoken to Jo about his "concern" nor taken any action against her. He said it just wasn't important enough to distract him from his otherwise busy schedule.

Rather than simply rely on my strong feeling that this so-called "drinking problem" defense could never be proven at trial, I decided to raise the ante. Because alcoholism—or even the mistaken perception of it—is a recognized disability under the Americans with Disabilities Act, we sought, and received, permission from the judge to add to

Jo's age discrimination lawsuit a claim for disability discrimination. This second claim for unlawful discharge could well result in additional compensation for Jo should the case be decided in her favor.

In an attempt to offset its blunder, the employer then sought refuge in a tactic currently much in favor among employment discrimination defendants, reliance on so-called "after-acquired evidence." This is evidence of misconduct that the employer learns of after the employee's termination, for which the employee would have been discharged had the company known of it during his or her tenure. In Jo's case, the company claimed to have found serious irregularities in her expense account reports, a favorite place to look for "after-acquired evidence" of misconduct. After I examined the expense reports of several colleagues and took several additional depositions (including that of Jo's immediate supervisor), it was relatively easy to demonstrate that the so-called irregularities were completely consistent with the procedure followed by Jo's co-workers.

The publisher then asked the court for the intervention of a mediator in an effort to reach settlement. (A mediator is a court-appointed person, usually a lawyer, who seeks to persuade the parties to enter into a voluntary settlement agreement. Unlike an arbitrator, a mediator has no authority to impose a settlement). Should the parties be unable to settle, Jo's trial should be scheduled early this year.

The permanent elimination of jobs for employees in their fifties, at a time when these same fifty-year-olds are healthier, more vigorous, and essentially younger than their counterparts of decades past, has placed employers and employees on a collision course that will have serious sociological implications for years to come, especially as that formidable group—the Baby Boomers—begins to approach the half-century mark.

While retraining in new skills is one widely discussed solution to the permanent elimination of traditional jobs, such training may well be too little and come too late to be of much help to today's unemployed fifty-year-olds. We face the real prospect of a disaffected large segment of our population, suffering widespread psychological and emotional upheaval, not to mention serious financial problems, as a result of age-motivated unemployment.

◆ ◆ ◆

Chapter 2

What Does Sex/Gender Have to Do with Your Job? Plenty: Sex Discrimination

Although there have been laws against employment discrimination for more than a hundred years in the United States, they varied from state to state. Not until some thirty years ago did Title VII (in addition to prohibiting discrimination based on race, color, religion, and national origin) establish federal uniformity, making it unlawful to discriminate against females—or, for that matter, males—on the basis of their sex. On-the-job gender discrimination occurs when an employee is treated differently from a person of the opposite sex under similar circumstances for reasons based solely on the employee's sex.

More Are Less Equal Than Others—Wage Bias

Historically, the most obvious example of sex bias has been paying women less than men for doing the same work. Although unlawful, the practice is pervasive, and even now, after years of strong feminist (and other) efforts to correct this inequity, women still earn only seventy cents for every dollar earned by men. This is *wage inequality,* not to be confused with the *glass ceiling,* which denies women the opportunity to *advance* up the corporate ladder (which also, of course, impinges on wage increases). Let's say you're a woman working as a publicity director for a large corporation, and you earn $35,000; your male counterpart, publicity director for another division of the same corporation, is earning $50,000. You and he have almost identical curriculum vitae—in fact, you went to the same college, worked together at another company, and then each of you got your "dream job."

Although you are worth as much as your male colleague in terms of employee value (or conversely, maybe he is worth only as much as *you*), nothing will be done to correct this unfair (read that *unlawful*) situation for two reasons, both very related:

1. Understandably, you don't want to quit your job— you love it, and protesting could lead to dismissal or, at the very least, rocking the corporate boat to your detriment,

                    and

2. Your company knows it can get away with such inequities.

So there you are: making seventy cents for every dollar your colleague makes. This goes on at every level of employment, from factory workers to upper-echelon managers. It's a sad, unlawful truth of life in the workplace. And, until recently, most women didn't challenge it because they wanted to keep their jobs.

Among the women who do take on such challenges, the litigant most feared by any employer is a minority female over forty years old. This is enough to make executives at even the grandest corporations quake in their boots because such plaintiffs fall into *three* categories protected by federal and state laws: age, sex, and race.

While women are victims of sex discrimination far more often than men, remember that if a male worker is treated less favorably than his female colleagues because of his sex, he has just as much a right to challenge this inequity. Here's a hypothetical example: A man is hired as an editor at a fashion magazine where all the other editors are women. Although he has similar editorial experience and a similar position, on the organizational chart, the female editors are making more than he is simply *because he's a man*. So workplace discrimination based on gender (sex) can work both ways.

Those who do fight for on-the-job equality may find themselves in double trouble: victims first of sexual discrimination and later of sexual harassment (which we'll talk about in the next chapter).

Ironically, some of the most frequently cited sources of gender bias occur in professions where women not only do the same jobs but also wear the same or similar uniforms as men: the military, police and fire departments. And often, female protests have less to do with wage inequities and more to do with the way they are perceived, or treated by their peers.

One New Jersey policewoman, for example, reported that in over five years with a local police force, officers on the midnight tour watched pornographic movies at the station house while she patroled the town—alone. Another policewoman reported that although she outscored two men on physical tests, and tied with another man on written tests, the men were hired promptly, while it took her five years (and a lawsuit) to gain her rightful place on the force.

Similar news reports show that women in the military are struggling for acceptance in what still seems to be a man's world. Two hundred officers in the air force, along with their supporters, have formed a group called WANDAS Watch (Women Active in our Nation's Defense, their Advocates and their Supporters). One target of their protests was the recently retired air force chief of staff, who had vocalized his opposition to women assuming increased roles in the air force. A few years ago he reportedly told a Senate panel he would "rather fly with a less-qualified male pilot than with a top-notch woman aviator."

Last year, when the first female astronaut to pilot a space shuttle successfully linked up with a Russian space flight, a group of former female pilots, thirteen women who called themselves FLATS (Fellow Lady Astronaut Trainees), recalled that when they had trained with NASA thirty years earlier, they were never called up as pilots. One FLAT, now sixty-five and a retired pilot, told the *New York Times,* "We could have done it, but the guys didn't want us." She remembered that one NASA official said at the time that he would "just as soon orbit with a bunch of monkeys than with a bunch of women."

In these "uniformed" cases, the problem is not one of wage or promotion, but of limited opportunities to perform the task for which these women were hired or were qualified to perform. The time-worn excuse of denying certain jobs to females in order to "protect" them from damage to their reproductive systems or possible harm to an unborn fetus has been held by the courts to constitute sex discrimination. Similarly, restricting the weight that females can be required to lift on a job or the number of hours they may work, in order to "protect" them (which obviously limits employment opportunities), also constitutes sex discrimination. In the same way, height and weight standards adversely affect job possibilities for women and are illegal unless it can be demonstrated that they are a *bona fide occupational requirement of the job*, that is, necessary for performance.

Speaker of the House of Representatives Newt Gingrich committed "verbal discrimination" while infuriating millions of men and women in 1995 when he said, "If combat means living in a ditch, females have biological problems staying in a ditch for thirty days because they get infections, and they don't have upper-body strength. I mean some do, but they're relatively rare. On the other hand, men are basically little piglets—you drop them in the ditch, they roll around in it, doesn't matter, you know."

Aside from Speaker Gingrich's skewed view, some common sense considerations should and do apply. For example, if a job at a trucking company requires lifting two-hundred-pound boxes for eight hours a day, an employer might justifiably refuse to give that job to a five-foot-two 110-pound woman (or man, for that matter). However, if the applicant could demonstrate that he or she could do the job, the employer would have no basis to deny it to him or her. As another instance, if a man is applying for a job as an attendant for the women's rest room in a restaurant or hotel, and is denied the job, that's not sexual discrimination; nor would a vice versa situation of a woman looking for a job as an attendant in a men's room be the case. In either of these examples, sex would be a bona fide occupational qualification.

If a woman has a license—and a desire—to drive an eighteen-wheeler, there's no *lawful reason* why she shouldn't have the job. If a man is licensed as a nursery school educator, there's no *lawful reason* why he shouldn't have the job. But stereotypical perceptions persist.

Shattering the Glass Ceiling

Another pervasive, insidious, and unlawful example of sex/gender discrimination in the workplace is the denial of promotional opportunities—the top jobs which women rarely attain. This is the "glass ceiling," a term that describes barriers women face in climbing the corporate ladder. One of my recent cases involved a trade association where a woman had held the post of executive vice president for eleven years. When the president retired, the trade group conducted a search for his replacement. The search committee sent a survey to all association members, asking for recommendations for the new president. The person most often named was my client, the executive vice president. We'll call her Doris. Disregarding its own members' choice, the association embarked upon an outside search, even hired an executive search firm, and not only did it *not* hire its executive V.P. for the position, it *never even interviewed her for it!*

The group has a hundred-year history—and all the former presidents were men. Previously, executive V.P.s—all men—had moved onward and upward to the presidency, but this was a precedent the board and the search team were now *not* following with my client.

When lawyers for the association told me we had "no

case," I could only wonder what law school they had attended and what cave they called home. In my opinion, this was one of the strongest cases of "glass ceiling" discrimination I had ever seen. There may have been some man as qualified as Doris, but she was the logical, painfully obvious choice for the job, which would have doubled her $100,000 annual salary. And even had the association located a more qualified male, there could be no excuse whatsoever for failing to at least consider Doris for the position.

The trade association argued that in its proposal given to the "search" firm, it stressed its willingness to hire a man *or* a woman for the position. But it turned out that of nine people interviewed for the job, seven were men; when Doris asked about this unbalanced proportion and the failure even to offer her an interview, she was told by the head of the search team that they were looking "for a suit," of course meaning a man. Eventually, the association offered the job to one man, who turned it down, and then they offered it to another man *with absolutely no experience in the business,* who accepted it.

The problem for Doris and others who find themselves in similar situations is that Doris was *still employed* at the trade association, and, of course, none of those board members, who chose to deny her even a chance of becoming president, made her workday any easier for her. To put it mildly, it was an uncomfortable situation. Not only were her superiors unhappy, but co-workers, fearful of incurring their boss's wrath, began to avoid her. Yet the story has a happy ending. We settled Doris's case, and she took a top job at another company that knew of her lawsuit and didn't hold it against her.

While it is certainly worse financially to be fired than to

be denied promotion, the decision to take legal action is, in fact, much simpler *if you've been fired*. The glass ceiling, remember, represents promotional opportunities, and that means if you want to sue it's almost certain that you will still be there! So consider the scenario. You're still going to be working for that same company. You'll be going to work every day, reporting to the same bosses who refused to advance your career. That's often an intolerable situation. I told Doris she would become persona non grata. She stuck it out, however, and ultimately prevailed.

Some glass ceiling crashes that have received recent attention in the press concern executives in areas where presumably *equal rights* would be in the forefront, such as the black women who feel they have been overlooked for promotion by their own associations, including the NAACP and the Urban League. People automatically and erroneously assume that because you're black or a woman, or belong to a certain religious persuasion, that you automatically favor those of similar persuasions—or at least treat them well—but this is patently *not true*. (Of course, in 1995, under a great deal of pressure to reform and reorganize, the NAACP ousted its former leader and did elect by one crucial vote Myrlie Evers-Williams, the widow of slain civil rights activist Medgar Evers.)

Sexual prejudice even exists in areas where one would like to believe that men and women are intellectually "liberated," such as college campuses. One friend of mine, who did not pursue a sex discrimination case, tells about her experiences as an adjunct professor at three different colleges. She truly wanted to build a career as a professor of creative writing, English literature, and broadcast and magazine journalism. And she had the appropriate credentials in all of these fields. Although she knew she had to pay her "dues" by teaching the early-morning or Friday classes, after three years she could not avoid the logistic or financial truth. Often the plum classes, when not taught by tenured professors, were given to young male graduate students with *no* experience, and despite her heavy course load, she realized she was earning only about five dollars an hour. "I thought these so-called intellectuals would be more intelligent about equal rights," she said. I told her, "People who discriminate are not necessarily stupid. They just discriminate."

Basically, the historical fact of life is that women were denied all types of opportunities for centuries—they didn't even get the right to vote until the Nineteenth Amendment was ratified by the states in 1920. (Ironically, one of the nation's strongest first ladies, Edith Galt Wilson, who actually performed most of President Wilson's duties while he recovered from a stroke, thought the vociferous suffragettes fighting for women's voting rights were, in her words, "distasteful," "unfeminine," and "disgusting.")

Even Jack Kennedy, whose election as thirty-fifth president of the United States was based so much on the efforts of female members of his family *and* his personal appeal to women voters (there were over three million more voting-age women than men in 1960—and female voters still outnumber male voters), had no real agenda for establishing women as equals in the workplace, or on other fronts. However, at the urging of a former "feminist" first lady, Eleanor Roosevelt, Kennedy did establish The President's Commission on the Status of Women, chaired by Mrs. Roosevelt, and by 1963 his administration had passed the equal pay law and the extension of the Fair Labor Standards Act. But as far as appointing women to high office in his administration, Kennedy fell significantly short of his predecessor, President Eisenhower. Since then, major strides have been made, but it would be disingenuous to pretend that decades—centuries—of ingrained second-class treatment of women has ended, and it will take more than federal or state laws to change this.

The Glass Ceiling Commission, established by Congress in 1991, recently published a report based on nationwide studies and research conducted by various industries. The report cites one study which noted that while women represent 46 percent of the labor force, they hold only 3 to 5 percent of senior management positions. Management jobs held by women are highest in social and health services and lowest in construction, engineering, and public utilities.

The glass ceiling is also crystal clear in the upper echelon professions of medicine and law. Thirty years ago, when I went to law school, maybe 2 or 3 percent of my classmates were women. In the ensuing decades, prestigious law firms across the country began to make concerted efforts to hire women. But today, despite the fact that law degrees are earned by almost as many women as men, there are very few female partners at major law firms, especially senior partners. That fact of life in the legal profession became very apparent to me when a female lawyer was referred to me by one of my former opponents in a discrimination case. (Sometimes clients come to you from the unlikeliest sources; in this case, actually, from the "enemy camp.") Sheila's complaint was that in the high-profile law firm where she worked, there were still very few female partners. She told me that the firm's rationale was that most women leave after five or six years *before* they reach partnership consideration levels, which takes about nine or ten years with the firm. But this is a self-perpetuating situation: Women leave law firms because they realize there are few if any female partners at their firm, and so they quit to establish their own practices or go on to other positions with better prospects for advancement. In the meantime, the law firms say there are no female partners because there is no pool to draw from . . . when actually, female lawyers have been discouraged from *staying* because there is no precedent, little history, and few incentives for them to stay.

About a year ago, I had an enlightening conversation with a female adversary who worked for a large law firm with a roster of stellar corporate accounts, one of whom was being sued for employment discrimination by my client. Perhaps to establish her own stature, she said early in our conversation, "I want you to know that I'm the only female partner in the firm's litigation department." When I responded that "Well, it sounds as if there may be some good sex discrimination cases at your firm," she didn't think it was funny.

Some might argue that when women reach a high position, they don't work quite as hard as they can to help other women who are trying to climb up the same ladder. But those who would say so should not overlook the former New York State banking commissioner who finally got the New York Stock Exchange to provide rest room facilities for women that are the equivalent of those provided for men. After months of lobbying without success, she finally threatened to rent a Portosan if the prestigious male-dominated stock exchange restaurant didn't build a ladies' room on the same floor as the restaurant. She got her rest room.

Going back to my earlier mention of the medical profession, in terms of high-level health care management, women have lodged some strong complaints about where they stand on the corporate ladder. For almost two decades, one notable group has fought for equal opportunities in a field dominated by their male colleagues. As one of its founding members, now chief executive of a top teaching hospital in New England, recently told the *New York Times*, "We were all working for new C.E.O.'s. *We* could be C.E.O.'s. But none of us was." The group had started off casually and informally, about a dozen women meeting over chicken dinner or Chinese food. They called themselves the A-Team, more than a little facetiously, and their target was to establish at least three of their members in executive suites within a few years, to deflate what they called the Old Boy Party. They have, by all reports, more than accomplished their goal. But, as noted in the *Times,* the need to establish such a group says a great deal about "the self-image of modern, professional women."

The Baby, the Parents, and the Corporate Scene

Having a baby or adopting a child should be one of the happiest occasions in life for parents. The federal government certainly did its part to make this a celebratory event by protecting the rights of new mothers with the Pregnancy Discrimination Act of 1978 (an amendment to Title VII), which provided that any employment discrimination because of pregnancy constituted a form of sexual discrimination. In other words, a woman's job should not, and cannot, be jeopardized because of pregnancy, childbirth, or parenthood. Accordingly, unless it can demonstrate a compelling need to replace you, your company is required to make reasonable efforts to hold your position for you during maternity leave. Although leaves vary from company to company, four to eight weeks is not uncommon.

But like too many things in life, protection by the law is no guarantee. Employers sometimes still discriminate on the basis of pregnancy. However, they can be made to pay the price for doing so. An example is my client Mary, a very successful national sales manager for a major apparel manufacturer. Upon notifying the company that she was pregnant and would be taking a maternity leave, Mary assumed that according to law and company policy, she would get her job back after the baby was born (at the conclusion of her leave). But, the day before she was due to start maternity leave, instead of a surprise party to celebrate her imminent motherhood, she was surprised instead with the announcement that she was terminated.

After considering her options (which are discussed further in chapter 6), Mary concluded that the only viable course of action was to sue for sex discrimination. Because the company could not offer a convincing explanation for discharging Mary, whose performance had been excellent, or especially a reason for the incredibly bad timing of her termination, her case was settled very favorably.

Understandably, her experience at having to bring suit left Mary—and other women who have been similarly mistreated—with bitter feelings. In Mary's case, all she wanted was the standard maternity leave that was her company's normal policy. It was her right to have it under the Pregnancy Discrimination Act, and the company's decision to discharge her instead turned a simple matter into a costly proposition for it.

Of course, if a woman wants more time than the company policy provides or considers reasonable, she runs the risk of losing the job protection provided by law. For example, asking for six months maternity leave would probably not be considered "reasonable" by most companies, particularly a small company, where such an absence could impose a severe hardship on company operations. You see, the company has rights, too. If legitimate business needs compel your company to hire a permanent replacement for you because it can't fill in with a temp or by having other people do your work, your right to reemployment will be affected. In such circumstances, the company only needs to offer you a position as equivalent as possible to your old job, or if there are none available, the company must only place you on a preferential hiring list for the first available vacancy for which you are qualified.

Such a worst-case scenario, of course, is less likely to happen in larger corporations because they have the ability to "cover" for an employee on maternity leave.

There is, however, a more subtle problem with having a baby than mere concern about your maternity leave. Sad but true, in the minds of many employers the far more significant consideration may be their concern for how well you will function as an employee *after* you return from leave, especially if you are an executive and your hours cannot be construed as working from "nine to five." Will you be willing, or able, to work as long or as hard? Will you *want* to do so with a little baby waiting for you at home? If the doubts are strong enough, the employer may look for an excuse to replace the new mom, perhaps with a male, or a single woman, or (entailing less risk for the employer) with another *mother* . . . but one whose children are old enough not to require the same attention as an infant.

Some women make their own choices, favoring mom status over job status. A former special assistant to the president, and deputy director of communications for national security policy, chose between "Barney and Bosnia" as she wrote in a "Hers" piece for the *New York Times Magazine*. When her son's first word was not *Mama* or *Dada* but *Beep, beep, beep* (referring to her White House pager), "I knew it was time to go." The choice for her was not as difficult as it is for others because she is confident she will be able to find other freelance or consulting work that allows her to care for her toddler, and keep her career irons in the fire.

Those women not able to make that same choice, financially or psychologically, often find that "motherhood" gives rise to a not-so-subtle form of discrimination, not only by their male bosses who are parents . . . but also, and perhaps more insidiously, by women who are mothers themselves. In Candide's best of all possible worlds, blacks would support blacks; Hispanics would champion Hispanics; Catholics (or Jews, or Muslim, or Baptists) would fight for their peers; and women . . . would support women. But it simply doesn't work that way. Women, with or without children, recognize perhaps better than men that a mother might be "distracted" by the birth of a child.

The thinking is that even if a new mother decides to return to work after four to eight weeks, she still will have her child very much on her mind and may not want to work the long hours that were customary in the past: "I'll put in my eight hours, but then I'm out of here." Frankly, many women *and* men don't see anything wrong with this. It's natural, normal, healthy. When I was working on Wall Street and my own boys were young, I wanted to get home to see them and spend time before they went to sleep for the night. As I see it, there's more to life than a job, but some employers have tunnel vision where this is concerned and have this great fear that parenthood is going to change *everything*—in most cases, it is probably blown way out of proportion, but it is something for the new parent to be aware of.

The clear reality is that many new mothers will have to conform to their employers' expectations, regardless of preference. Today a two-income family may often be as much a necessity as it is a choice.

I have a current case involving a woman with a good job. Gloria was a successful salesperson who had what she thought was an excellent working relationship with her superiors. Then she became pregnant, and suddenly unusual situations started to occur. Her supervisors weren't "totally satisfied" with her memos on particular accounts; they said maybe she wasn't working hard enough; in small but significant ways they began to pressure her . . . and continued to pressure her, and it was having an effect, mentally and physically. Then Gloria had a miscarriage. When she returned to work, her bosses, who were both women with children, really weren't very sympathetic about her personal tragedy. Some months later, she got pregnant again, and once more, they made her working conditions miserable. Finally she uttered what they probably considered the magic words: "I quit."

Ordinarily, if you quit your job voluntarily, you're on your own and waive such benefits as unemployment compensation and health insurance. However, if your employer has created intolerable working conditions, under which neither you nor any reasonable person in your situation could do her job, your resignation can be considered a "constructive discharge," which is the legal equivalent of being fired. (We'll discuss constructive discharge at greater length in chapter 6.) Some months later, after the birth of her son, Gloria asked me to represent her. At a hearing before New York State's Human Rights Division, Gloria's supervisors offered a number of defenses, including predictably, "We have children . . . we work . . . we're in exactly the same position . . . we wouldn't discriminate on the basis of motherhood."

Turning their argument around, my point was that "the fact that you know what the pressures are on a mother with a young child demonstrates that you're in a better position than most to worry that a new parent may not want to work long days, and fear that her interests may focus more on family than on a career." I did not suggest that this was true in Gloria's case, or for that matter for other new mothers. My point was that the problem existed in *their* thought processes, and because of the timing—getting tough on Gloria both times she became pregnant—their motives were suspect. Gloria's case is still pending.

Job discrimination as a result of impending parenthood affects other workers, too: fathers and adoptive parents. Even though men don't get pregnant (aside from the Arnold Schwarzenegger movie *Junior*), taking care of newborns (or, for that matter, children of any age) is no longer viewed as "women's work." To that end, early in his administration, President Clinton spearheaded passage of the Family and Medical Leave law, which provides for time off—without pay—to help care for a new baby or an ill family member. The new law, which went into effect in 1993, helps prevent discrimination, but there are no available figures indicating how many new fathers take advantage of it. Or how tolerant employers are toward proud new dads who feel that celebrating a baby's birth means more than passing out cigars.

Until the enactment of the family leave law, adoptive parents had no uniform legal protection for their jobs after taking time off to care for an addition to their family. Although some states in fairness had recognized this fact of life and passed laws safeguarding jobs while adoptive parents took a leave, traditionally, there had been a distinction between protection provided for natural birth parents as opposed to adoptive parents. Many employers would provide maternity benefits for a natural baby but not an adopted one, which made little sense. All new babies need special care, no matter how they join a family. Now fathers, as well as mothers, of natural or adopted children, are covered by the federal Family and Medical Leave law.

New York State passed its Adoptive Parents Child Care Leave Act in the late 1980s, guaranteeing adoptive mothers times off equivalent to that afforded natural birth mothers in the form of maternity leave. If a natural mother is entitled to eight weeks "maternity" leave, so is an adoptive mother.

In 1991, Grace, a New York personnel executive, asked me to handle her case. She had requested time off to adopt a child and was flatly turned down. Her bosses told her unequivocally she had no right to a leave to adopt a child. Clearly they were not aware of the New York law. They got a very rude legal awakening when they had to settle with Grace for a substantial sum for denying her leave. This situation serves to reinforce the importance for companies—even the large conglomerate that employed Grace—to keep current with labor laws.

Clearly, getting the laws passed may be the simplest part of the whole equation. Most disputes arise when people try to circumvent the laws. And there are vigorous arguments being waged as to whether, even in 1996, there are gaps in the federal and state laws against employment discrimination. A hot topic is homosexuality. Is it, or should it be, a protected workplace characteristic? Even Speaker Gingrich, who seems to have a "solution" for everything, was somewhat at a loss for words when confronted with a demonstration for homosexual rights that included his sister Candace. Gingrich avoided any mention of his position on gay rights and said, "I never mix politics with family."

Protecting Job Rights of Homosexuals

In the last decade, the subject of homosexuality, euphemistically termed "sexual preference," has garnered an inordinate amount of public and media attention, mostly, perhaps, because of the AIDS epidemic. Gay rights activists have generated banner headlines and made social and legal strides, even though some of their activities to generate publicity (such as interfering with Catholic masses) were considerably more notorious than meritorious. Hidden behind or beneath the headlines though were the cases in which gay men and women simply wanted an opportunity to perform their jobs and live their lives. Many were (and are) not activists. Some who had decided to come "out" found that they had to "come out fighting" to protect their basic opportunity to work at a job and earn a living.

Who can forget Tom Hanks and his Oscar-winning role in *Philadelphia*? Although the protagonist won a Pyrrhic victory (just before he died of AIDS), it was not because he had been discriminated against because of his sexual preference. The suit that was brought under the ADA succeeded because of the individual's *disability*—AIDS. Had the fired lawyer in the case based his suit solely on being fired because he was a homosexual rather than on having AIDS, he would not have won his case. Pennsylvania, like most of the country, has no law protecting homosexuals from workplace discrimination. Only eight states—California, Connecticut, Hawaii, Massachusetts, Minnesota, New Jersey, Vermont, and Wisconsin, plus the District of Columbia—have statutes protecting the employment rights of gays and lesbians. So do a handful of cities: New York, Philadelphia (now), Denver, and Pittsburgh, to name a few.

In 1994, Senator Edward Kennedy launched a program to sponsor job protection for gays on a federal level. As of now the proposed legislation has been put on a back burner, and the chances of it moving forward are slim, given the prevailing conservative tenor of Congress. (Remember Representative Dick Armey's "slip of the lip" in calling Congressman Barney Frank, "Barney Fag"?) One reporter suggested that one way for Armey to prove he is not a bigot would be for Barney Frank, who is now shepherding Kennedy's bill through the House, to offer Armey cosponsorship of his bill to end discrimination against Americans based on their sexual orientation. So far the bill has 139 sponsors. It will take many more votes to get the legislation through Congress. As a flip side to that coin, currently the Supreme Court is reviewing whether a 1992 amendment passed in Colorado depriving homosexuals of protection from discrimination is constitutional or not. (Individual Colorado cities, such as Denver, Boulder, Aspen, and Telluride, do have laws protecting homosexuals, but there is no statewide law.)

Actually, unlike the United States military, where homosexuality was grounds for discharge (since softened to "Don't ask; don't tell"), most companies do *not* have written-in-stone rules about hiring or firing men or women because of their sexual preferences. But they do have *unspoken rules*. In a New York city case, for example, an engraver at a posh Fifth Avenue jewelry store sued the company for $96 million, charging he was a victim of sexual discrimination. The engraver's colleagues were using binoculars to check out the models at an agency across the street. When the engraver refused to take part in this voyeurism and reported it to his supervisors, his co-workers called him a "faggot." Although his supervisors clamped down on the Peeping Toms, they demoted the engraver to part-time work, instead of giving him the promotion he deserved after twenty-two years of employment. Now, this case is interesting because the engraver is *not* gay . . . but he allegedly suffered discrimination because his co-workers and bosses thought he *was*. Perceptions, again.

In another case, chronicled in *The New Yorker* by best-selling author James B. Stewart *(Barbarian at the Gates)*, a management consultant (CPA) in Pennsylvania (which, as noted, has no state statute prohibiting discrimination because of homosexuality) was fired without severance pay and medical benefits because of his activities on behalf of gay rights. (For several years, the CPA had signed an employment contract that allowed termination because of homosexuality.) When he tried to establish his own business, his former boss sent letters to potential clients saying "It's well known that homosexuals are significantly at risk for AIDS." The CPA sued his former boss and *lost;* in fact he had to pay his ex-employer over $100,000 in damages because he had solicited the business of the former employer's clients in violation of the clause in his contract forbidding him from doing so.

The court dismissed the CPA's claim of "wrongful discharge": "The argument that a person is protected in Pennsylvania from either being a homosexual and announcing it in public, that may be the law someday. Someday the legislature may create such a set of legal principles. But as I understand the law to be at this point in time there is no such protection." Although an appeal of the CPA's case was rejected by the A.C.L.U., the Lambda Legal Defense Fund, which defends homosexual rights, agreed to take the case. The CPA lost on appeal by a split decision. The majority of the panel of judges ruled in favor of the former employer because the former employer's offensive, but not illegal, firing of the CPA because of his homosexuality did not excuse the CPA's attempt to garner the business of his former boss's clients.

In another high-profile case, perhaps one might conclude that justice was well served. A high-ranking Vietnam veteran nurse, who was discharged in 1992 during a security clearance interview after admitting she was a lesbian, had her day in court . . . and in the media. The nurse was ultimately reinstated, and although her televised story received less than rave reviews, it did make some important points about discrimination against gays in the military. The officer who discharged the nurse said, "As soldiers we have to follow our orders whether we agree with them or not. Now the defense has presented a case arguing that this policy is wrong. I . . . have not made any argument that the policy is right. I don't have to. The policy is there, and the policy is clear."

Perhaps there's something upbeat to be said about this case. Although the nurse was initially punished for being open about her sexual preference, which she described as not much different from being born left-handed, she was ultimately reinstated. Most gay men and women cannot claim such successes, unless they can qualify for legal redress because of sexual harassment or under the protective umbrella of the ADA, which we'll discuss in subsequent chapters.

There's still one more avenue that might provide legal protection. As mentioned earlier, about one-third of the states have "wrongful discharge" or "abusive discharge" laws, which decree that unless an employer has a valid reason to fire you, he can't do it. This is in direct contrast to the laws in the remaining two-thirds of the states, where an employer can fire you "at will," for any reason—in those states, you can be terminated for a good reason, a bad reason, or *no reason*—as long as it is not a reason protected by federal or state laws against employment discrimination.

To many, it will seem that there is something terribly wrong with allowing an employer to fire an employee because, for example, he or she revealed to the authorities that the company was doing something unlawful. It's like "mom and apple pie." How could any court deny redress to an employee (sometimes called a "whistleblower") who is merely doing his civic duty? In those states where courts have upheld the employment-at-will doctrine, their explanation for so doing has generally been that it is not up to the courts to write new laws but rather it is the obligation of state legislatures to enact them.

Although these states have been reluctant to move in this direction, some headway has been made. In the late 1980s, for example, New York carved out an exception to "at will" employment for those who blow the whistle on actions or conditions that present a hazard to the public health and safety. While this is a pretty narrow exception, and there have been few cases brought under it, in 1994 one nurse who exposed misconduct at a large hospital and was fired for her efforts, was awarded $750,000 in damages.

But getting back to discrimination because of sexual preference, let's say you live in one of the states where they have a wrongful discharge law, like New Jersey. If you're fired there but you prove "I've done a good job, I have good performance reviews, everyone liked me, but my employer fired me because I'm gay," that might constitute wrongful discharge. So, depending on where and what the manifestations of homosexuality may be, there may be laws that provide redress—but at this time, there are no existing federal employment discrimination laws. In fact, as noted earlier, there seems to be a trend toward legislation in the opposite direction.

◆ ◆ ◆

Chapter 3

Don't Just Deal with It: Sexual Harassment

During 1994 and 1995 sexual harassment graduated from boutique status as a form of employment discrimination to superstardom as the headline of the week. To some extent this notoriety was generated by high-profile table-turning harassment cases in which *men* were the victims.

Who could forget the mega exposure over the movie *Disclosure?* One columnist described Michael Douglas as "the poster child for sexual harassment." Other writers and broadcast commentators, from movie reviewers to political pundits, pontificated on the significance of this role reversal. *Disclosure* was seen in some circles as "politically correct," especially when Douglas announces, "Sexual harassment is about power." The film was also depicted as a wake-up call to a pervasive workplace hazard; even author Michael Crichton, who started the ball rolling with his 1994 novel *Disclosure,* on which the film was based, declared that placing a man in a situation women have had to put up with for years helps Americans understand the plight of women who are harassed. If that's so, it's a rather sad commentary on employers' recognition and enforcement of what, after all, are federal laws prohibiting such actions.

Actually, Crichton got the inspiration for his novel from a real-life story in which the "stars" were not nearly as glamorous as Michael Douglas or Demi Moore. The male victim, now thirty-four, began a new job as a division manager for a California hot tub manufacturer in 1986. His female boss, now forty, a mother of two, first offered helpful suggestions, then offered romantic suggestions, which escalated to hugs and kisses and more. When he gave in, she was pleased with his work; if he resisted, she found fault with his job performance. In 1988, the boss came to his house and refused to leave until they had sex. He capitulated, reluctantly. But he didn't resign because "I loved my job. I was paid well, over $40,000 a year." However, in 1991, when he married his fiancée, the harassment got "100 percent worse." He was demoted, insulted, and threatened with dismissal.

He quit his job in 1992 and filed a sexual harassment suit against the company. In May 1993, a Los Angeles jury awarded him $1 million, which a judge then reduced to $350,000. Both sides are appealing, but unlike the Douglas role in the movie, our harassee has not worked since he resigned and is seeing a psychiatrist. In an interview with *The National Enquirer,* he said, "I'm convinced there are thousands of men out there in the workplace being sexually harassed every day. . . . It was pure humiliation."

Among those thousands are eight men on the opposite side of the country who call themselves the Boston Eight and have filed sexual harassment charges against a leading weight-loss company. The men claim that at the firm, which is predominantly staffed with female supervisors and colleagues, they were denied promotions, subjected to embarrassing comments about "tight buns," and were forced to perform such demeaning acts as shoveling snow (which, apparently, is in the same vein as women making and serving coffee to male supervisors). The Massachusetts Commission Against Discrimination is currently mediating the case.

Even before hearings were scheduled to settle the complaints, the aggrieved victims told *Time* magazine they were "shocked" to be exposed to off-color comments, and after their terminations, they immediately hired a team of women lawyers *and* a public relations agency. Since male sexual harassment suits are definitely in the minority, when the Boston Eight's case was spilled to the press by the PR agency, it received instant, nationwide, *mega* media attention: the *Wall Street Journal* ran a front-page story; bookers from the "Today" show, "Entertainment Tonight," "A Current Affair," and others fought to schedule these newsworthy guests.

I mentioned earlier that the unusual twist of men as victims of sexual harassment accounted for some of the inordinate amount of attention this form of job bias received in the last two years. The rest of the attention was generated by *only a handful of women,* among the thousands of cases brought before the EEOC or state agencies. In 1989, only 6,000 harassment cases were registered with the EEOC. Then sexual harassment, which has always been a problem, and which many women "just dealt with," came to national (probably worldwide) attention with the Anita Hill–Clarence Thomas controversy. (Ironically, until 1989, Thomas chaired the EEOC, and perhaps not so ironically, under his leadership age, sex, and other employment discrimination cases were routinely postponed, contributing to the backlog mentioned earlier.)

According to Anita Hill, writing in the *New York Times* in 1994 about the Thomas case and the Paula Jones accusations against President Clinton,

> In 1991, the issue and the surrounding circumstances caught society by surprise. The general public was unaware of harassment as a legal question. ... The [Thomas] hearings touched deep feelings about power, race, and sex—complex, volatile emotions that came together on television as a real-life story. For many the impact was astonishing. ... Among women, the reactions were quick, almost instinctive. Women had not often spoken publicly about sexual harassment until then, but by doing so during and after the hearing they educated society. By talking about their own painful experiences, they showed how pervasive the problem is, while explaining why they have been reluctant to raise claims.

The news stories, from Anita Hill to the present, convey the shock stuff of what sexual harassment involves.

One significant after-effect of the Thomas-Hill hearings was the resignation, in late 1995, of Oregon Senator Bob Packwood. After more than three years of investigation, the Senate Ethics Committee voted to expel Packwood from the Senate, according to one committee member, for "a systematic abuse of women, power, and this Senate."

Unquestionably the harrassment allegations made by nineteen women, some dating back a quarter of a century, were very damaging and required some sort of Senate censure. But would the censure have been as extreme had the investigation not begun on the heels of the Thomas-Hill controversy? Democrats and Republicans alike (and polit-

ical commentators on both sides) agreed that pre–Thomas-
Hill, or perhaps some time in the future, Packwood might
have survived, but he was doomed in this super-sensitive
time frame.

While women activists in and out of the Senate won
their battle against Packwood's sexual abuses, they lost
one of the Senate's strongest proponents of women's rights
legislation. Ironically, the decision to expel Packwood
probably had less to do with his sexual abuses than the prevailing political climate. Packwood's Republican colleagues
didn't want to risk the spectacle of public hearings (which
Packwood ultimately asked for) to investigate charges
against him in a crucial pre–presidential-election year . . .
and his Democratic colleagues welcomed the opportunity
to reduce the number of Republicans in the Senate.

Here's how the EEOC defines sexual harassment.

Unwelcome sexual advances, requests for sexual favors, and other verbal or physical conduct of a sexual
nature constitute sexual harassment when (1) submission to such conduct is made either explicitly or
implicitly a term or condition of an individual's employment, (2) submission to or rejection of such conduct by an individual is used as the basis of
employment decisions affecting such individual, or
(3) such conduct has the purpose or effect of unreasonably interfering with an individual's work performance or creating an intimidating, hostile, or offensive
work environment.

In other words, harassment can take two forms. First, the
quid pro quo situation in which submission to the sexual
advances of a superior is a term or condition of employ-

ment (being hired, getting promoted or staving off discharge). In Hollywood, this used to be called the "casting couch syndrome." The other form of sexual harassment exists when a hostile work environment, which unreasonably interferes with the victim's job performance, results from the offensive sexual conduct of the company. The factors determining whether a hostile work environment exists are psychological harm, severity and frequency of the offensive behavior, and whether the conduct is verbally humiliating or physically threatening.

The standard applied by the courts in determining the existence of a hostile work environment are twofold: (1) does the victim view it as hostile, and (2) would a reasonable person perceive it as hostile. As previously discussed, under the law, both males and females may be sexually harassed by a supervisor of the opposite sex or even by persons of the same sex. Employers may also be held responsible for sexual harassment by customers and nonemployees; this is termed "third-party harassment." (As a rule, in order to sue for sexual harassment of any type, the victim must first make the employer aware of the harassing circumstances and give it an opportunity to remedy the situation.)

Unfortunately, the murky waters of on-the-job sexual offenses become even murkier when a woman—and it usually involves women—has to stave off the sexual overtures or insults of a client she knows is economically important to her company, the so-called third-party harassment. One woman I represented in this type of situation worked as an account executive at a well-known public relations agency. Cindy was an attractive divorced thirty-seven-year-old with a young son. Her major account was a nationwide retail organization. Over the course of several months Cindy was subjected to offensive behavior by a senior vice president for the retailer, about which she complained several times to her supervisors at the agency. Among her charges: the V.P. made frequent remarks about Cindy's sexuality, in her presence and to others during meetings; he defamed her by telling people at his company and hers false stories about her prior romantic relationships with business colleagues and others, even claiming that Cindy had had an abortion. Faced with the choice of offending an important client or sweeping the matter under the rug, the agency fired Cindy. Its reason? Complaints of poor performance by the harasser himself.

Needless to say, Cindy was devastated by the entire experience. She was emotionally battered and drained by the harassment, the loss of her job, and the damage to her fifteen-year career and reputation in the industry. She really couldn't decide whether to sue or just try to forget the whole ordeal. In the end, with the support and encouragement of her family and friends, she decided to fight back. Because Cindy had the good fortune to have female coworkers who came forward to verify her complaints and confirm that they, too, had been on the receiving end of similar behavior by the senior V.P., it became powerfully clear to the agency and the retail organization that they would lose at trial. Therefore, they settled on terms very favorable to Cindy.

While Cindy's case received local media attention, two other sexual harassment cases in 1994 and 1995 received coast-to-coast coverage. The first was a case on which I did some expert commentary for the cable channel Court TV. It involved the forty-year-old secretary who filed harassment charges against the world's largest law firm, with

1,700 attorneys and offices in thirty countries. She worked for the firm for only a few weeks, during which time one of the firm's partners made sophomoric off-color remarks to her about sex and her anatomy, and on one occasion patted her breast pocket in what he described as a search for candies. She quit and sued.

At her trial, the legal secretary produced testimony by other former female employees of the law firm, lawyers and support staff alike, that they had complained of misconduct by the partner. When the senior partners conceded that they had merely "slapped [the offender] on the wrist," their fate was sealed. After a lengthy trial lasting several weeks, the jury awarded the secretary a fairly modest $50,000 in compensatory damages. In my opinion, this properly reflected the short duration of her employment, and while not discounting the offensive nature of it, the almost pathetic behavior of the partner, who could probably use professional psychiatric help. However, the jury also awarded a record-breaking $7.1 million in punitive damages against what it obviously viewed as the real culprit, the law firm itself, which had essentially condoned its partner's conduct by, in effect, turning a deaf ear to earlier complaints of sexual harassment.

As noted earlier, *compensatory damages* includes payment for loss of income and other lost financial benefits, such as insurance or pension, along with payment for pain and suffering; *punitive damages,* which are damages meant to "punish" the employer/offender, are awarded, among other reasons, based on what the jury thinks the defendant can pay, as well as on what will act as a deterrent to future misconduct. In other words, the bigger the company involved, the greater the punitive damages. After the record-setting punitive damage award to the legal secretary, several jurors said they based their decision on the law firm's disclosure that it distributed $189 million to its partners and had net profits of $65 million in 1993. As one juror concluded, "A tithe is 10 percent."

It is unlikely that the legal secretary will see that $7 million-plus award any time soon; appeals may go all the way to the Supreme Court. Although the award may be reduced along the way, it will be difficult for the law firm to have it voided. After the decision in her favor, the victor said, "I felt vindicated. I hope it will make a statement to all employers that sexual harassment cannot be condoned or tolerated."

The second record-breaking award centered around the Tailhook case. Navy and marine aviators annually hold what is called the Tailhook Convention, and for years the preferred location was a hotel in Las Vegas. (In 1994, after all the "dust" had settled, or was being settled, the convention was held in San Diego.) In 1991, according to news reports, the convention fun and games got out of hand, and ultimately more than eighty women claimed to have been assaulted or molested at the convention. But one woman, a former navy lieutenant who first settled her claim out of court with the military for an undisclosed amount (and then was forced to resign from the navy, thereby forfeiting her career), went on to sue the hotel chain for its breach of security. She testified that she had been trapped in the hotel's third-floor hallway one night during the convention by a group of men who shoved their hands down her bra and tried to reach up her skirt and pull off her underwear.

The former lieutenant was awarded $1.7 million in compensatory damages and another $5 million in punitive damages when the jury ruled that the hotel had failed to provide adequate security at the convention. (The punitive damages were subsequently reduced by $1.5 million to reflect sums received in her settlement with the military.) "I think justice was served," she said. "This sends a message that you can't tolerate abusing women, even for making money."

The *New York Times* reported in a lead business story in July 1994, "Although many companies have long ignored sexual harassment . . . several legal trends—most arising after the celebrated Clarence Thomas hearings—have raised the costs so much that still neglectful corporations may be courting economic disaster." From 1992 to 1993 awards in sexual harassment cases increased 98 percent to $25.2 million, according to the EEOC; no figures are available for 1994, but with the inclusion of the awards in favor of the navy lieutenant and the legal secretary, which we discussed, it is likely that those figures would double again.

While these are awards to *single* individuals, the same *Times* story also details the high costs of "class action" suits, in which several individuals band together to sue a company. In one recent class action case, a fast-food restaurant chain paid $132 million, including legal fees and court costs, to workers charging harassment. In another case, in April 1994, a grocery store chain settled a sex-bias case for more than $107 million.

The fast-food case may have inspired a recent spate of suits across the country, involving waitresses and female bartenders, whose uniforms and demeanor may be considered fair game for flirtatious customers or supervisors. These men or women should think again. For example, finding strength in numbers, four waitresses at a well-known bar-restaurant in California sued one male manager and one female manager for "fondling, pinching, kissing, and generally harassing" them. In this suit, a famous actor who learned what he termed his "flashy bartender moves" from the bar-restaurant's employees in preparation for his role in a film gave a sworn statement about the "restaurant's environment."

On Long Island, three former waitresses and a current one working at another restaurant chain charged that "male supervisors fondled and groped them." In one case, it was charged, a man pried open the legs of one waitress and repeatedly thrust his pelvis against her. In another instance, a supervisor reportedly told a waitress she got good tips "because she went under the table to give customers oral sex," according to the complaint.

Complaints of sexual abuses are rampant in all areas of the workplace. Here are some other current cases.

◆ The executive director of the NAACP was forced to resign after charges that he spent $332,400 of organization funds to keep a female employee from filing harassment charges against him.

◆ A New York City policewoman filed harassment charges against her sergeant, who referred to her as a "bimbo," "bitch," and "skirt." She also said she suffered severe retaliation for more than a year for complaining to her superiors.

◆ The chairman of a major industrial supplies company is being sued for $21 million for assault and harassment by two former housemaids.

◆ One of the nation's major advertising agencies' general

counsel, a lawyer who presumably should have known better, took an "indefinite leave of absence" after being targeted for harassment charges by female employees.

However, perhaps the case with the most impact has been the one in which the president of the United States is the man being sued. Shortly after Paula Corben Jones initiated her suit against President Clinton for an alleged forced sexual encounter in May 1991 (while he was still governor of Arkansas), she earned this blaring headline in *The New York Post*:

PAULA: I'LL PUT PREZ' PRIVATES ON PARADE

Nice alliteration. But more important, it serves to highlight the potential for abuse in such publicity-garnering, reputation-damaging cases. When Jones originally filed her claim against the president in the spring of 1994, many observers, who may or may not have had political axes to grind, immediately compared it to the Anita Hill charges against Clarence Thomas. But there was a very big difference: Hill was not looking for personal or monetary compensation when she testified before Congress. Whether she was believed or not, she simply testified to her knowledge of Thomas's behavior. She did not seek, nor did she obtain, big bucks by doing so. On the contrary, among some groups she was excoriated for her efforts.

On the face of it, Paula Jones cannot be credited with the same lofty motives. Since her claims became public, she has been all over the media. In some cases, on national television, she seemed to undergo a complete transformation of image and character (appearing very demure for an interview with Diane Sawyer on "Prime Time"). Jones has stated that she wants to give any money she makes from her $700,000 suit (or any revenue that might come her way through publicity) to charity, but she has never specified numbers or names.

Her own relatives have called her "loose and lascivious" (according to many news reports), and more recently, with her original flashy makeup and demeanor back in place, she has, as noted earlier, declared she had "foolproof evidence" that President Clinton made sexual advances toward her three years ago: "a description of Clinton's genitals . . . I have the proof . . . and I want the opportunity to be heard." And then some of her own private parts—nude photos taken of Jones in 1987—were recently revealed in *Penthouse* magazine.

After Paula Jones filed her suit, articles pro and con appeared in record number, some of them, obviously, politically driven and opportunistic in terms of skewering Bill Clinton to yet another wall. But much of the national correspondence reflected thoughtful letters from women who had themselves been harassed and compared the Anita Hill case to the Paula Jones case. One woman, writing to *New York* magazine, said, "After losing three of the best jobs a woman could ever have during the sixties because of sexual harassment, I believe I qualify as an expert on the subject. I believed Anita Hill. I could empathize and feel her frustration and pain. Paula Jones, on the other hand, does all women a disservice. Any woman with a lick of common sense knows why she's being invited to any man's hotel room. Does Jones expect us to believe she went there for a

Gideon Bible reading? This is why women's causes get nowhere. There is always some conniver trying to get hers on the backs of the true victims."

But it is not only Paula Jones who is keeping the Anita Hill–Clarence Thomas controversy alive. The charges still have a life of their own, as it were. In late 1994, Jane Mayer and Jill Abramson, former writers for the *Wall Street Journal,* published *Strange Justice: The Selling of Clarence Thomas,* which included interviews corroborating Hill's charges and other material damaging to Justice Thomas. The book opened old wounds and stirred up pro and con commentaries in media ranging from the *Wall Street Journal* and the *New York Times* to such popular venues as *People* and ABC's "Turning Point." Did he or didn't he? . . . may never be resolved.

While the Jones suit has been put on hold—in December 1994 a judge delayed the trial until after President Clinton leaves office—other litigants have also tried to cash in. How about the $8 million suit against TV host Bob Barker by Dian Parkinson, a former hostess on "The Price Is Right." Barker admitted he had sex with Parkinson but said that it was consensual. Parkinson's claim was soon followed by that of another model on the show, alleging similar abuses. First a judge dismissed the "wrongful termination" claim from Parkinson's suit, denying her charge that she was forced to leave her job because she withdrew her sexual favors. Then a few months later, Parkinson dropped the remaining claims because her doctor "advised that I am not strong enough to see this thing through." Her dropping out means that a jury will not have the opportunity to decide whether Parkinson's charges were legitimate, represented "wishful thinking," or were seen as an easy way to become rich overnight, legally. In the meantime, Bob Barker is still waiting for an apology from his former employee, and has threatened his own suit for "malicious prosecution."

There is also a relatively new phenomenon beginning to emerge with scattered cases involving *same gender* sexual harassment. In one major city, for example, a female law secretary sued her female attorney boss because the woman "continually made sexual advances toward her." The secretary said her boss would "eye her body up and down in a lewd way," and comment on how "sexy" she looked. Allegedly, the boss would press her chest against the secretary's back, would discuss male semen and engage in other "sexually inappropriate and offensive behavior."

In a Pennsylvania case, a homosexual successfully sued his gay boss for "unwanted sexual attention." As the story was recounted on "Donahue," the supervisor had frequently discussed sexual acts, told off-color jokes, made indecent gestures and inappropriate physical contact, and suggested job favors in return for sexual favors. When the employee didn't acquiese, the boss retaliated.

Whatever the legal grounds behind such cases, there is no denying that as we approach the end of the twentieth century, sexual harassment claims are on the increase, and society, the legal system, and employees and employers alike will have to confront the issues, the legalities, and the possibilities of major settlements.

Of course financial compensation is important, but when a person is not hired, or is denied a promotion, or is fired or forced to quit a position because of sexual harassment, the emotional result can far exceed any financial losses. The greater loss is that of confidence or self-esteem. The feeling that "maybe I provoked this," or "I can't take care of my-self," or "I can't provide for my family," is drastic, devastating. And, as I've said before, this "emotional distress" must never be taken lightly.

Are such cases getting out of hand? Are women (and in some instances, men) blowing the whistle too soon and at great expense for sexual slights that may not be as important as the lawsuits say they are? That's a hard one to call, and many experts disagree on just where one draws the line between innocent flirtation and sexual harassment, not to mention opportunism. A family physician, writing in the *Los Angeles Times,* says, "We do seem to be overdoing it a little when it comes to taking offense from certain words, gestures, and touches. (Rape is a crime of a totally different dimension and is certainly not to be considered in the same arena as sexual harassment.)"

While media attention to sexual harassment cases continues to build, there are also some generational considerations that apply. Older women, for example, might be less likely to sue for what they still call "flirting." And they might be more worried about losing their jobs over such a suit. Younger women seem more militant and possibly less frightened to complain about employers or co-workers who make any "moves" on them.

The headlines may make it seem as if sexual harassment is a new variation of "fun and games on the job." It's not. Sexual harassment is age-old and worldwide. It was chronicled in Europe for centuries in cases where schoolboys were seduced by their teachers, or landowners exercised *droit de seigneur* (the right of the master) with housemaids. Sexual harassment occurs today in high-tech Japan, which aside from its centuries-old tradition of geishas, now has a twenty-first-century spin on treatment of women. Commuting for hours to and from jobs is a fact of life in Japan, but according to the Associated Press, some male commuters make their time more pleasurable by fondling female commuters. The fondlers, or gropers, have become so prevalent they even have a nickname, *chikan,* which means "idiot man." One woman's group in Osaka, Japan's second largest city, says that 75 percent of women in their twenties and thirties who responded to a questionnaire reported having been fondled by *chikan* at least once. One unrepentant groper has even written a best-selling book on the subject: *A Groper's Diary* has sold over 75,000 copies since it went on sale in 1994. The author boasts that he molested *about a dozen women and girls a day for twenty-six years!* He says he counted on women being too embarrassed to cry out and said in an AP interview, "I wouldn't try groping in the United States, because American women seem too tough. But Japanese women tolerate us—or I'd be in jail by now."

Chapter 4

Ready, Willing, Able to Work: Disabled but Capable

It was one of those "first the good news; now the bad news" times that happens to all of us. The good news for this woman was that on a Monday, in mid-1994, she had her hand shaken by, and picture taken with, President Clinton, providing a "photo op" and story for broadcast and print media. She was one of three New Yorkers the president met with who had written letters to him about health care. During her meeting with Mr. Clinton, she said she was one of those Americans who had fallen through the health insurance net: She lost her insurance when she was terminated from one job and her insurance at the new job wouldn't begin for three months. In the interim, she had discovered a lump in her breast and couldn't afford to see a doctor.

The following day, she told co-workers at the real estate management firm where she worked as a bookkeeper all about her meeting with the president. Then, at the end of the day, she was fired. Her boss told her she wasn't "performing to his level of service," that he would pay her for the entire week, but she shouldn't return to work.

Attorneys for the company insist that this bookkeeper was fired for "performance" and that they had no idea about her physical condition, which seems questionable, based on the widespread coverage of her meeting with Mr. Clinton. In her view, she was fired because of the potentially high medical costs for treating what might have turned out to be cancer. Fortunately, a hospital in suburban New York offered to diagnose and treat her condition, and another company immediately scheduled her for a job interview.

This incident reveals a very alarming and sad truth. All too frequently when employers discover a worker has a potentially costly or disabling illness, termination for "poor performance" is the medicine of choice from the management point of view. Similarly, a worker who is already disabled may arbitrarily be denied employment or a promotion because the employer worries about the insurance expenses, or about the capability of the employee.

In an ideal world, such workplace discrimination *would never occur*. In a realistic world, such discrimination *should never occur*. But it frequently does. During the last four decades, many states enacted their own laws protecting the disabled; then the federal Rehabilitation Act of 1973 extended protection to handicapped persons working for federal contractors, or organizations (such as schools, libraries, local governments) that received federal financial assistance. Finally, in 1991, the Americans with Disabilities Act (ADA) was passed, providing broad, uniform federal safeguards for the disabled.

While the ADA now covers a wide spectrum of physical and mental disabilities, the move to gain civil and employment rights actually began over thirty years ago by those who were *physically disabled*. Because California has always been a trendsetter in social action, it is not surprising that one of the major efforts to achieve rights for the disabled began at the University of California at Berkeley. In the fall of 1962, a young quadriplegic, paralyzed as a result of polio, attended his first day of classes. To get there he had to be carried up dozens of stairs in his wheelchair, and despite being dependent on "the kindness of strangers," he viewed this as his first day of freedom. The student and his followers were determined to challenge the widespread belief that the disabled were incapable of joining the social mainstream—going to school, holding jobs, taking care of themselves. They took on the banner of disabled rights with the same fervor as those groups working for civil rights during the 1960s.

These disabled colleagues founded the Rolling Quads and then, with a modest federal grant, established the Physically Disabled Students' Program, which helped students get to class and provided emergency wheelchair repair services. In the early 1970s, they also started the Center for Independent Living, with a goal of helping the disabled find jobs and homes, offering services to graduates with disabilities in the Berkeley area. Their efforts were so successful that today there are three hundred centers from coast to coast. In 1975, the former Berkeley student, who successfully earned his degree, became director of the California Department of Rehabilitation, which only a decade earlier had claimed it would be impractical for him to attend college and ultimately work full-time.

This group of pioneers seeking rights for the disabled has had many significant triumphs—not just socially, but also psychologically. One of the group is publisher of the disability magazine *Mainstream,* which urges people to "claim their disability, to feel okay about it." In an article in *Modern Maturity,* this disabled writer minimizes the achievements of those she calls "super-crips," the paraplegic who climbs a mountain or the blind sailor whose goal is to cross the Atlantic Ocean alone. She and the other pioneers focused on alleviating the *ordinary* challenges that make it difficult for the disabled to lead useful, productive, satisfying lives. Another writer, who formerly edited *The Disability Rag & ReSource,* compares the rights and fights of the disabled to the fight for gay rights, and points out that there's nothing to be ashamed of regarding either condition.

Yet another longtime supporter of the California group, who sued the New York City Board of Education twenty years ago when, because of her disability, she was denied certification to work as a speech pathologist, is today a United States assistant secretary of education, whose responsibility is supervising programs for special ed, rehab, and disability research.

While the initial leadership corps may not have been all that large, their actions affected many. *Modern Maturity* quotes a figure of forty-nine million disabled men and women. A Louis Harris study sponsored by the National Organization on Disability revealed that two-thirds of men and women with disabilities ages sixteen through sixty-four are *unemployed.* Almost 80 percent of those surveyed want to work; they do not want to collect welfare or disability benefits. Those who do hold jobs often earn less than their co-workers and are bypassed for promotions. To be sure, some are born with disabilities or encounter them because of illness or accidents early in life, but many more problems manifest themselves with advancing age. According to the 1990 census, 12 percent of our population, or about 31 million people, are 65 or older, and more than half have disabilities or illnesses that affect their daily activities, including sensory disabilities (eyesight, hearing) and physical disabilities (illnesses or physical limitations).

The irony is that as more and more disabled workers are ready, willing, and able to work . . . and as more and more workers with diagnosed but treatable and manageable illnesses or medical conditions are ready, willing, and able to work . . . the more employers tend to deny them jobs or promotions because of perceived performance problems and possible hikes in their already astronomical company health insurance costs, or simply terminate them from jobs for the amorphous reason of "performance." Significantly, from mid-1992, when the ADA law went into effect, until mid-1994 more than 25,000 disability discrimination claims were filed with the EEOC, *most occurring after employees were terminated.* According to *Longevity* magazine, the twelve health categories that triggered the most disability discrimination claims at the EEOC are pregnancy, back, neurological, emotional-psychiatric problems, heart problems, extremities problems, HIV/AIDS, vision problems, hearing disorders, substance abuse, cancer, and asthma.

I wish I could note a reversal of corporate attitudes, even those evolving simply as a result of compliance with federal laws. But this is not the case. The situation will probably get worse before it gets better, as increasing numbers of workers rely on their rights under the ADA. How encompassing are these rights?

The ADA protects individuals with disabilities, who are otherwise qualified for the job in question, from discrimination based on their disability. The law defines disability as a physical or mental impairment that substantially limits one or more of the major life activities of an individual.

This includes physiological disorders or conditions, cosmetic disfigurement, anatomical loss affecting the sense organs, neurological, musculoskeletal, speech, respiratory, cardiovascular, reproductive, digestive, genito-urinary, hemic (blood), lymphatic, skin and endocrine body systems. It also includes mental and psychological disorders, and those caused by substance abuse and dependencies on legal drugs.

Excluded from the protective arms of the ADA are homosexuality, bisexuality, exhibitionism, transsexualism, transvestism, and pedophilism, but as noted in chapter 2, a homosexual (or heterosexual) suffering from AIDS cannot be terminated for this illness, since it is construed as a disability.

The ADA also stipulates that ordinary physical characteristics that are within normal limits do not constitute a physical or mental impairment. For example, a worker can't charge he or she has been discriminated against because of eye or hair color, right- or left-handedness, other physical characteristics, or personality traits *that fall within the parameters of "normal."*

In addition to protection from discrimination based on disability, the ADA prohibits discrimination against persons who have *recovered* from a disability (such as a mental or emotional illness, heart disease or cancer). This is particularly important today because, as we'll discuss later on in this chapter, in too many instances confidential records about a worker's health history find their way into management hands and lead to unlawful termination.

Aside from having a disability or having had one in the past, the ADA also protects persons who do not have a disability, never had one, or have a disability that does not

substantially limit a major life activity but who, nevertheless, are *perceived* by an employer as having a limiting impairment. An example of this might be a man or a woman
who does not "look healthy," perhaps because he or she is
very thin. While perfectly capable of performing the duties
of the job they hold or are seeking, the employer, suspect-
ing illness, denies them the job.

The opposite can also be true. Take the case of the
woman who was fired from her job as an attendant at a
state institution for the mentally retarded in New England.
A doctor for the state told her in 1988 she was too fat to
return to a job she had held twice before. Despite her weight
(at five-foot-two she weighed 320 pounds), she said, in an
interview with *People* magazine, "I had a spotless record.
I was dumbfounded and hurt." Her cause was championed by the American Civil Liberties Union, which sued the
state on her behalf. In 1993, a U.S. appeals court upheld a
lower court decision that awarded her $100,000 in back
pay, plus compensatory damages, and ordered her reinstated to her job. The judge rejected the state's argument
that the woman's obesity was a "voluntary condition," not
a disability. He ruled, in what may have legal precedent,
that "morbid" (or severe) obesity could be regarded as a
disability, and people who suffered from it should be protected under federal law.

And in 1995, a California jury awarded one million dollars to a man who claimed that he had been fired by an auto
parts store because he weighed 400 pounds. In this case,
the judge ruled that obesity is a physical disability rather
than a matter of overindulgence and that the auto parts
worker was protected under state and federal law.

In one of my cases that is still pending, my client's disability, although apparent to her doctors, was denied by her employer. Sarah, who worked as a middle manager for a federal agency, was diagnosed with "bi-lateral trochanteric bursitis," a painful condition affecting her neck, upper back and shoulders, which was often exacerbated by long hours at the computer. Her physical condition was made worse by her two immediate bosses, who made improper remarks, treated her shabbily, and generally created emotional stress that triggered the onset or worsening of the physical symptoms of her illness. The federal agency's physician, concurring with the diagnosis of Sarah's personal physician, placed Sarah on disability leave, recommending rest as the best treatment.

While on leave, the bursitis attacks abated and Sarah's health improved to the point where her doctor said she could go back to work, so long as she was transferred to a different job where she wouldn't be pressured by her two nemeses. Under the ADA, this would be considered a request for a "reasonable accommodation to a medical condition," which companies are obliged to comply with when possible. But senior management at the agency refused to grant Sarah a transfer. Totally disregarding the fact that Sarah's request was based solely on the medical advice of her doctors, their attitude was that the agency would not allow Sarah "to pick and choose" her assignments, as if she were acting on some whim. Following her doctor's advice, Sarah said she could not and would not jeopardize her health by returning to the same old job. The agency said she would be fired if she didn't come back. When Sarah held firm on her doctor's advice, the agency fired her (while she was still on medical leave) without consulting its own doctor, who had *exclusive* authority to place employees on, and remove them from, medical leave (which according to agency policy is granted to an employee only if he or she is disabled).

Sarah consulted me, and we sued; our position was that the agency failed to make a reasonable accommodation for her disability as required by the ADA. The agency sought to trivialize the complaint by describing Sarah's claim as being based on stress, which is not considered a disability under the ADA.

The agency filed a motion for summary judgment. As will be explained in greater detail in chapter 6, in summary judgment motions a party to the lawsuit alleges that the essential facts of the case are not in dispute and that, applying applicable law, the case should be resolved in its favor by the judge. It is a procedure for terminating the judicial process without the need for a jury trial. Because I agreed that the essential facts were not in dispute, and the case could be resolved by the judge on the basis of the existing law, we cross-moved for summary judgment. Unfortunately, it has been many months since these motions were filed. The judge on the case is immersed in a very long, drawn-out, high-profile criminal trial and has yet to make a decision. We continue to wait. In the meantime Sarah went back to school to pursue a new profession in which she is now employed.

While Sarah's medical condition was obvious and verified by her doctors, as was that of the overweight auto parts worker and the overweight mental institution attendant, in many other cases, no physical impairment is visible. The employee's disability becomes known to the employer through channels that should have been (and were thought to be, on the part of the worker) *confidential*.

For example, not long ago I handled separate suits for two employees of a leading communications company, both of whom were fired for what ultimately was demonstrated to be reasons of disability discrimination. Joseph, fifty-two years old, with a long record of success in his field, had worked at the company for only five weeks as the publisher of a trade magazine when he was discharged for "incompetency." Firing this vigorously recruited publisher before his desk chair was even warm raised my suspicious antenna in an eye blink, particularly when I learned that his bosses had actually only observed him in "action" for three or four days, during which he never had the chance to show what he could do.

But most suspicious actions have a reason, and if you look hard enough, you can find it. My research revealed that what really happened was that midway through his brief tenure Joseph applied for a company life insurance policy. On the application, he revealed that he had a heart condition, for which he had been hospitalized twice in the past. Instead of being safeguarded in a confidential employee insurance file, this information found its way from the human resources department to the company's executive vice president. The company never submitted Joseph's life insurance application for processing; instead, two weeks later he was fired. When I learned that the company was self-insured (meaning it paid employees' medical bills rather than their being paid by an insurance company such as Blue Cross/Blue Shield), I knew I had discovered the real motive—getting rid of an employee who posed a potentially expensive health risk.

The company made the usual motion for summary judgment (in the hope of avoiding a jury), requesting that the case be dismissed on two technicalities: (1) Joseph's heart condition did not constitute a recognized disability under the ADA, and (2) the company president who actually fired Joseph had no personal knowledge of his heart condition. The judge promptly denied the motion, concluding that heart disease is clearly a disability covered under the ADA. He also found actual knowledge of Joseph's heart condition by the company president was unnecessary because, in deciding to fire Joseph, the president had relied on the untrue and unfair performance evaluation by the executive vice president, who was well aware of Joseph's disability.

The trial, which came a few months later, was one of the more unusual ones I have been involved in. Actually, it was fairly routine until the jury began its deliberations. As we sat in the courtroom, after four days of trial, awaiting the verdict, we could hear the jurors (one in particular), who were in the adjacent jury room, shouting at one another. Then juror number seven (reflecting the seat that she occupied in the jury box) began sending notes to the judge saying she was tired and wanted to go home. The judge denied the request, but the notes kept coming, increasingly desperate in tone. Finally, at 9:30 P.M., the judge sent the jury home for the night.

When jury deliberations resumed the next morning, the shouting and notes to the judge from juror number seven continued until the marshal (a court officer who is in charge of the jury) reported to the judge that juror number seven was threatening to bite and kick a fellow juror who was refusing to go along with the views of his colleagues. Concluding that juror number seven was mentally unbalanced, the judge dismissed her from the jury and instructed the remaining jurors to continue their deliberations.

At 7:30 P.M. that night, the jury reported that it was hopelessly deadlocked. So the judge had no choice but to discharge the jury and declare a mistrial. By talking to the jurors afterward, we learned that it had been hung five to one in favor of Joseph. Before juror number seven was discharged, the vote had been six to one in our favor.

Although a retrial was scheduled to begin a short time later, it never took place because the company settled. It recognized that it had "dodged a bullet" by very narrowly escaping a verdict in Joseph's favor. On the day before the retrial was to begin, the company, sensing that it would not be as lucky the next time, made an attractive settlement proposal, which was accepted by Joseph.

Incredibly, this wasn't an isolated case within the same publishing company. Three weeks after Joseph was dismissed, Ted, the thirty-three-year-old advertising director —the number two position after the publisher—(married, and the father of a young child) was diagnosed with leukemia. When this was discovered, again through improperly channeled health records that should have been confidential, the company relieved Ted of his duties as advertising director, assigned them to a less-qualified subordinate, and demoted Ted to the position of salesman. Ted felt he had no choice but to resign and retain my services. So I was representing both Joseph and Ted simultaneously. I have rarely, if ever, seen as blatant and obvious a case of discrimination as that suffered by Ted.

We immediately filed a disability discrimination suit on Ted's behalf and, amazingly (perhaps through the intervention of some higher power), a trial was scheduled for only six months after the filing date. As indicated throughout this book, six months from filing to trial date is virtually unheard of in scheduling a trial, but it was really needed in this case. Ted had undergone a bone marrow transplant and was not getting better fast. Despite the early trial date, he could not have endured the strain of testifying. We decided it was in his best interests to use the impending trial as leverage to reach a settlement. Ted wanted very much to force the company to admit its discrimination and to have something to leave his wife and child if things didn't work out for him.

Recognizing its great vulnerability at trial and not fully appreciating the limitations on Ted's ability to testify at the trial, the company was eager to settle, and it did. While the settlement was certainly respectable, if I had the luxury of more time, we could really have socked it to them. But Ted was happy with not only the financial outcome, but also the fact that he felt vindicated. Sadly, Ted passed away only a few months later.

Clearly, privacy and confidentiality in the workplace are major issues of the late 1990s, when an employee's life history (and even lifestyle) can be as readily available for viewing as his or her work history. Usually, it's only a matter of pushing the right computer keys. Although the ADA mandates that information from an employee's preemployment physical must be separated from personnel files, there is no prescribed procedure by which employers are required to separate such information. (Incidentally, under the ADA, an employer may not ask about the existence, nature, or severity of a disability and may not conduct medical examinations until after the employer has made the applicant a conditional job offer. Once a conditional job offer is made, an employer may make disability-related inquiries and conduct a medical examination, if it does so across the board for all applicants in the same job category.)

Your company's job manual may state, for example, that the results of your physical are confidential, and are only to be used for purposes related to insurance. But the possibility remains that your physical report may find its way into your on-the-job background, and could work against you. In the same way, insurance claims for medical treatment or tests, which should also be maintained separately, can end up in your easily accessible personnel file.

And, believe it or not, it can get even worse. You may think that what you do or say on your own time is your own business, and none of your employer's. However, increasingly, it can become Big Brother's business too, to borrow a term from Orwell's *1984*. Beware what you convey or transmit over E-mail or through your computer, because Big Brother may be watching over you. According to a report in *Money,* your company may be monitoring what you do *after* nine to five and could eventually use such habits or lifestyle practices against you. Only three states—New York, North Dakota, and Colorado—have statutes protecting employees from job discrimination based on any legal activity you choose to engage in after work. Moreover, in half the nation's states, the only outside-the-job activity for which an employee is protected from discrimination is smoking!

And twenty-two states have absolutely no lifestyle protection laws at all. This means that in most of the country, your company can use what you do on your own time to determine how well you perform your job (read that: whether it wants to continue you in its employ) . . . whether

it's drinking six martinis before dinner . . . or riding your
Harley-Davidson . . . or taking herbal medications for your
arthritis, which may label you as a "health nut" . . . or even
seeking counseling to get through a bad relationship, or divorce, or the death of a mate. If your company doesn't approve of your lifestyle, your job may be in jeopardy.

An even more insidious situation can arise if your employer is one of the over 80 percent of major companies that
offer wellness programs, or EAPs (employment assistance
programs). These ostensibly altruistic programs are supposed to provide free counseling to help employees work
out personal or family problems. And they are supposed to
be confidential. However, if an employee is asked to sign
a release waiver, and later down the road applies for
worker's compensation or sues for "wrongful termination," that supposedly confidential information may come
back to haunt him. Let's say an employee has a problem
with alcohol that affects his health but not his job performance. Although alcoholism is considered a disability
under the ADA, he might be better off seeking help from
AA, which is indeed anonymous, than confiding his problem in an employer-sponsored counseling program. Or take
police departments, which all have counseling programs in
place to assist members of the force with the considerable
stress placed on them by their duties. It is no secret that cops
frequently choose not to avail themselves of this service in
the belief that whatever they may confide can and will be
used against them in pursuing their careers.

Some efforts have been made on the federal level to control such confidentiality leaks, but so far nothing mean-
ingful has been accomplished. The Privacy for Consumers
and Workers Act, sponsored by Senator Pat Williams (D.

Montana), which would curb electronic monitoring (via phone or computer), seems to be in limbo, or may have been shelved entirely. Another Senate bill, introduced in May 1994, the Health Care Privacy Protection Act, sponsored by Patrick Leahy (D. Vermont), which would establish limited access to medical information with penalties of up to $250,000 and/or ten years in prison for releasing private medical details for personal or vindictive motives, may have suffered the same fate.

Unquestionably, major legal strides have been made in protecting the civil rights of the disabled. Companies that not only comply with the law but are willing to give disabled workers a *fair* chance to succeed, whether they are wheelchair bound or bound by limitations resulting from mental or physical problems, are the good guys in the story. But there are also the bad guys—and it takes more than laws to correct the unfair employment practices. It takes groups like the Center for Independent Living and its leaders and people like the overweight mental institution attendant, the obese auto parts worker, Joseph, Ted, and Sarah to challenge unlawful discrimination and pave the way for others who are, after all, "ready, willing, and able" to be productive workers.

◆   ◆   ◆

Chapter 5

Discrimination Based on Race, Religion, and National Origin

Affirmative action (the use of goals, special recruitment efforts, set-asides, or quotas to increase job opportunities for minorities and women), which for decades was a positive force for combating discrimination, has now in some quarters assumed a less-than-favorable connotation. Suddenly in 1995, an approach to equal employment opportunity that was taken for granted came under critical scrutiny on many fronts as to whether it works, whether it's fair, whether it's legal, and, in the final analysis, whether such programs should be preserved as they are, modified, or most drastically of all, completely eliminated. Affirmative action became a major issue in the 1996 presidential election.

Having discussed the legal prohibitions against making employment decisions based on an employee's age, sex, or disability, we will now address the remaining characteristics that cannot motivate employment decisions: an employee's race, religion, and national origin. For a change, let's put the cart before the horse and look first at the unique way our country has sought to combat discrimination against minorities.

Where and when did the concept of affirmative action originate? The answer is the United States Constitution, which guarantees equality for *all* men and women. In other words, this great document, on which the fundamental rights of all Americans are based, envisions a color-blind world. "Color-blind," as an expression for total equality, was first used one hundred years ago, in 1896, by Supreme Court Justice John Marshall Harlan. Refusing to accept segregation on Louisiana's railroads, Harlan, in a dissenting opinion, wrote: "Our Constitution is color blind. In respect of civil rights, all citizens are equal. The law regards man as man and takes no account of his surroundings or his color." Half a century later, Thurgood Marshall (then a prominent civil rights attorney, and not yet a Supreme Court justice), arguing before the Supreme Court in the landmark case *Brown* v. *Topeka Board of Education,* reaffirmed the notion of a color-blind Constitution in attacking school segregation by declaring "distinctions made on a racial basis or on the basis of ancestry are odious and invidious."

But despite the Constitution, its Fourteenth Amendment, and the words of Harlan and Marshall, such "odious and invidious" distinctions were all too prevalent. You don't have to be a social scientist to know that in too many instances, minorities, particularly blacks, historically have been less equal than other Americans. President Lyndon Johnson's plan for a Great Society tried to remedy the effects of two hundred years of slavery, followed by decades of second-class citizenry, by giving blacks a boost to make up for lost time. This "boost" in the mid and late 1960s, labeled "affirmative action," established special treatment remedies, from Head Start programs all the way through to employment advantages. The programs were further championed in the 1970s—perhaps surprisingly—by Richard

Nixon, as a way of eliminating blatant bias and opening the doors to blacks, women, and other minorities.

Affirmative action was, and is, an exception to the Constitution, because rather than treating people *equally,* it treats minorities *more favorably* than others. However, this well-intentioned exception to "color blindness," created to remedy the present effects of past discrimination by giving advantages to particular groups, has always had an inherent problem, one that now has assumed far greater impact than in the past: Conferring special treatment on one group, of necessity, is at the expense of another group.

Assuming there are a finite (limited) number of jobs, in a color-blind world blacks, who represent 14 percent of the population, should get 14 percent of jobs. But if the government decides it wants blacks to get 30 percent of the jobs to make up for all those years when they got far *less* than their 14 percent, this means nonminorities are now getting only 70 percent of employment opportunities, instead of their proportionate 86 percent. This disproportionate ratio seemed okay in better economic times: There were enough jobs to go around, the economy was growing, and few people felt the negative impact of policies and programs preferring minorities over whites. Now with jobs "going south" (being permanently eliminated), the adverse impact of affirmative action is much greater. Because nonminorities are feeling the job denial pinch as never before, they have become far less tolerant of affirmative action.

This frustration with what is now known as "reverse discrimination" led to a major referendum in that most populous and frequently trendsetting state, California. In 1995, two conservative academics presented a plan called the

California Civil Rights Initiative, scheduled to be on either the primary ballot in March 1996, or the ballot for the national election in November. The plan, which calls for a return to a standard of "true color-blind fairness," reads: "Neither the State of California nor any of its political subdivisions or agents shall use race, sex, color, ethnicity, or national origin as a criterion for either discriminating against, or *granting preferential treatment to,* any individual or group in the operation of the State's system of public employment, public education, or public contracting."

This is a very subtly written, smartly worded initiative. How can anything be wrong with a proposition that simply mirrors the Constitutional mandate that everyone is to be treated equally under law? Predictably, the California referendum is very attractive to voters—73 percent of them, mostly white voters, according to current polls—but the effect of the referendum essentially blows out affirmative action, an exception to the Constitution, *entirely.* (Significantly, the state of Washington recently proposed a law similar to the California initiative.)

The "frustration" underlying support for the California initiative is starkly reflected in the statement of one San Francisco firefighter, who told the Associated Press, "Everybody falls into one or even more than one protected class. That is, everybody except white males. We're hiring tiny women. Size is no longer a criterion." But, he pointed out, equality or diversity "doesn't carry grandma down the stairs in the middle of the night."

In 1995, reverse discrimination was also the issue when the Supreme Court heard arguments in the case of a white subcontractor from Colorado who submitted the low bid to erect guardrails on a federal highway but lost out to a construction company owned by a Latino because the white general (primary) contractor got a bonus for awarding the subcontract to a minority-owned company. The Colorado subcontractor said, "I'm not mad at minorities, but I don't feel the government should be encouraging discrimination. This has been happening to me for fifteen years and I don't see it ending."

The Colorado subcontractor's case was considered to be a potential vehicle for the Supreme Court to dismantle government programs that steer contracts to "disadvantaged business enterprises," such as those owned by black Americans, Hispanic Americans, Native Americans, Asian Pacific Americans, other minorities, and women. And in a 5-to-4 decision, which dealt a severe blow to affirmative action, the Supreme Court did rule that most federal programs that set aside contracts for minorities and women are unconstitutional. "Federal racial classifications, like those of the state, must serve a compelling governmental interest and must be narrowly tailored to further that interest," wrote Justice Sandra Day O'Connor.

But the issue is not going to disappear. While the Supreme Court deals with affirmative action and reverse discrimination in a manner consistent with the views of the Republican Congress, President Clinton, spurred on by women, minority, and Democratic lawmakers, has defended affirmative action. Thus, the three branches of government are on a collision course of monumental proportions.

Clearly it is a mistake to assume that the groundswell against reverse discrimination engendered by affirmative action is simply a good faith effort to ensure equal rights for persons of any race, color, or religion. In fact, this is a very hot political potato. The adverse impact of most affirmative action programs falls most heavily on blue-collar white males, formerly known as Reagan Democrats. Their discontent undeniably contributed largely to the big Republican election win in 1994.

Some of the political challenges to affirmative action programs as we go to press are:

◆ Shortly before announcing his candidacy for president, *Senate Majority Leader Robert Dole* asked the Congressional Research Service of the Library of Congress to prepare a review of all federal legislation that supports affirmative action "preferences," also euphemistically called "compensatory opportunities." The report showed there were about 160 different programs. Speaking about affirmative action in general on NBC's "Meet the Press," Dole, still the presidential front-runner, asked, "Has it worked? Has it had an adverse, a reverse reaction? Why did sixty-two percent of white males vote Republican in 1994?" He answered his own question: "I think it's because of resentment of things like this, where sometimes the best-qualified person does not get the job because he or she may be one color. And I'm beginning to believe that may not be the way it should be in America," he said. "We did discriminate. We did suppress people. It was wrong. Slavery was wrong. But should future generations have to pay for that? Some would say yes. I think it's a tough question."

◆ *Senator Phil Gramm,* another Republican presidential contender, pledged that if he's elected, *on his first day in office* he would end certain major set-asides and other affirmative action programs.

◆ A third Republican presidential candidate, *Lamar Alexander,* said "I hope to play an active role in supporting California's initiative."

◆ Presidential hopeful California governor *Pete Wilson* ordered an end to all statewide affirmative action programs not required by law or court decree.

◆ *Speaker Newt Gingrich,* the undeclared presidential candidate, promised that as soon as the GOP's Contract with America was enacted, the next target would be affirmative action. He will work to "zero out" appropriations for selective programs. Although President Clinton would probably veto any bill to eliminate affirmative action *totally,* he can't veto individual appropriations. *If there's no money appropriated, there's nothing to veto.*

◆ Even though President Reagan's cabinet and major advisors declined to end affirmative action programs, as did President Bush, *President Clinton is once again on the hot seat.* While he is committed to continuing affirmative action, he also says what the country needs "is a civil conversation on what could be a potentially divisive issue," and has called for "an intense, urgent" review. President Clinton's description of the affirmative action challenges facing America is "mend it, don't end it."

◆ *Jesse Jackson and other black leaders* adamantly insist that affirmative action programs stay in force.

◆ *New York's Senator Daniel P. Moynihan,* who helped invent the policy in 1965, says it may now be causing more harm than good and that maybe the time has come to take another look at the broader issues.

In my view, Senator Dole is correct in terming this issue "a tough question." It is indeed. Because the viability of affirmative action is tied directly to the economic health and well-being of our country, it should be viewed as a fluid rather than static concept. It *must* roll with the punches (be adjusted as the economic climate dictates). The solution is not to abandon affirmative action and its successes because times are tough, but to scale back to insure the fairest possible treatment to *all* workers.

So, the battle lines are drawn. Idealistically, affirmative action would have righted all the collective discrimination wrongs committed by society . . . but it hasn't worked out that way. Some opponents say what has happened is nothing more than promoting *tokenism*. In any event, when evaluating the conflicting positions on affirmative action, one might do well to heed the old Latin admonition *Caveat emptor,* let the buyer beware; or in this case, *Caveat voter,* let the voter beware.

While there is no easy solution, maybe 160 federal laws supporting affirmative action are too many. Some of these laws have existed for thirty years. But at what point do they stop? At what point do Americans and Congressmen and state officials and Supreme Court judges decide that enough effort has been made to remedy the wrongs committed by our ancestors? And how far do we extend these protective and beneficial preferences? Do Hispanics, or Asians, or other immigrants who have not been mistreated during our country's history deserve the benefits originally meant for blacks? When the pie is shrinking, problems magnify.

Who will protect the rights of the white construction worker whose family is going hungry because a minority worker has gotten his job . . . not because he's better qualified, but simply because he is black or Hispanic or Asian? When feeding your family is the issue, concern for preferential rights goes out the door. If you start with the premise that *any discrimination* is wrong, then you cannot say that the victim of reverse discrimination has no rights.

Newspaper and magazine columnists of every political stripe have also commented on these developments. And even the most politically progressive called for some modifications in what was a good program that may have outlived its original beneficent intentions. Pete Hamill, who has spent his career championing the rights of the underdog, wrote: "Affirmative action should be reformed, not destroyed. It should be based on economics and class, instead of race or ethnicity. The poor of all races need to have the chance to move up. Poor blacks and Latinos should forge a coalition with the children of Sicilian bricklayers and Pakistani cab drivers and Russian garment workers. The laws of affirmative action . . . can help to open doors. Once in the room no law can help. But the chance to walk through that door is part of the American promise. It should not be thrown away in a national tantrum."

Syndicated columnist Joan Beck brings up the point I mentioned earlier. Should "Hispanics and other recent immigrants to the United States—many of them or their families here illegally—be entitled to preferential treatment over whites just because they are minorities? Blacks, in

particular, resent immigrants being counted toward affirmative action goals."

While the commentators comment, and the politicians
pontificate, reverse discrimination cases continue to
emerge. A white coach in Long Island claims he lost his job
to a black coach; a white teacher in New Jersey, with credentials equal to a black teacher, lost out in a job struggle
where there was only room for one of them. In mid-1995,
the federal Justice Department, acting on a case referred by
the EEOC, sued a major university for running an affirmative action program that refused to hire white men as
janitors. An assistant U.S. attorney general said of that suit,
"Cases involving employment discrimination against white
men are rare, but no less important than cases involving minorities and women."

Blacks and Hispanics also resent being tokenist pawns.
Listen to one Hispanic woman: "In watercooler talk, I'm
a twofer. That's a person who fits into two so-called protected classes under affirmative action laws: a woman and
a Hispanic." Myriam Marquez, a columnist for the *Or-
lando Sentinel*, wrote that she first found out about her
unique title when she asked a professor about a career in
journalism. "You're a twofer," he told the Florida writer.
"It's a plus that you don't have an accent, and you don't
look like a minority." Marquez writes, "Here we are, thirty
years after [affirmative action], so what do we have? We
have onefers and twofers and nofers, and a hell of a lot of
resentment on all sides." Although she agrees there are
good reasons to have some type of affirmative action, she
concludes: "What the creators of those programs didn't anticipate, however, was the resentment and ambivalence

that many of us who have benefited from affirmative action feel. For every opportunity I get, there's a forced recognition: I'm a twofer."

Well, while the political and sociological battle regarding the pros and cons of affirmative action rages on, there are still legal battles to be fought. One of the biggest cases I ever handled, quantitatively speaking, was on behalf of ten black police officers against the city that employed them. My clients alleged that they had been denied promotions and better assignments because they were black. Almost all of them had advanced education: some were currently in college, others were college graduates, one was in law school, and one had a master's degree. Despite their education and proven on-the-job performance, any promotions and better assignments (such as plainclothes) were v-e-r-y slow in coming . . . if they came at all.

The ten officers, who were a clear and noticeable minority on the police force, retained me to represent them in their suit before the New York State Division of Human Rights. Although they were able to joke about their situation, unquestionably these police officers were upset about how they had been treated. Not only were their qualifications as good or better than those of their white colleagues, but in many cases, they had *better* credentials than their *superiors*. The case moved slowly from filing to finish. Months were spent on investigations and hearings, along with numerous adjournments and postponements. But a funny thing happened on the way to judgment. During these delays, one by one, my clients were promoted and given better assignments. One sergeant became a lieutenant, a couple of others who had been second-grade detectives were booted up to first-grade status, another who had been denied promotion to sergeant suddenly got upgraded to that rank; and others "miraculously" got the plainclothes assignments they had been seeking.

In a relatively short period, then, all these seemingly impossible "dreams" came true. After years of stalling, postponements, and the like, by the time the New York State Division of Human Rights was ready to issue a decision, there was no longer a dispute to be resolved . . . it was *moot*. We lost the battle but won the war. *We won by losing* because the wrongs had been righted, all my clients had, in fact, *been promoted* or awarded the better assignments they had been seeking. Ordinarily, there are three possible outcomes to litigation: win, lose, or settle. But the city that employed the policemen came up with a *fourth alternative*: right all the wrongs, and then there is no discrimination for which to be held accountable.

However, because the "winning" police department really didn't feel great about the cost of its "victory," it kept a close eye on my clients, hoping for the commission of some infraction that would give the department an excuse to withdraw some of the assignments or promotions. As a result, my relationship with some of the police officers didn't end when the trial ended. One of the officers, who had been transferred from uniform to plainclothes duty, and who had been the most vociferous of the ten in demanding his rights, actually turned out to be a time bomb waiting to explode. And when it happened, he played right into the police department's hands. Shortly after the case was concluded, Carl got himself in trouble. He was brought up on charges of having an affair with a white female police dispatcher who claimed she overdosed on cocaine that she had gotten from Carl. Carl denied the charges and asked me to defend him at a departmental hearing.

It looked like a tough case until I got the opportunity to cross-examine the dispatcher, who had taken to glaring at me as she testified. So I returned her glare with one of my own and eventually asked her if she was a habitual drug user. Naturally she said no. Trying to look disconcerted at her denial, I next asked whether she had ever used cocaine. Again, she said no. Then, manifesting the best expression of desperation I could muster, I said, "Well, have you ever seen cocaine?" Smugly, she replied that she had not. So I snapped the trap shut and said, "If you're not a user, and you have never seen cocaine, then how do you know that what Carl gave you was cocaine?" She had no response. Her inability to properly identify the substance she had inhaled rendered her testimony "hearsay" and thus inadmissible.

On this basis, I made a motion to dismiss the case against Carl. The hearing judge said, "Let's have a conference." I declined, saying, "The alleged victim can't even identify this drug as coke. There's no case." The judge suggested settlement—suspension of Carl for three months, rather than discharge. We declined the offer, telling the judge he had no choice but to throw out the case. The judge pulled me aside and, revealing what could only be seen as his own personal bias, tried to persuade me with the argument that "this kind of person" would only get into trouble again, so it would be a good lesson for him. I insisted that the case be dismissed. And it was. Was this all a setup to get Carl because of his strong support for the earlier discrimination case? Probably, but we'll never know for sure.

It seems that there is something about uniforms and employment discrimination (don't forget our earlier discussion about sex discrimination in uniformed jobs). In a recent "60 Minutes" report, statistics showed that four out of five Japanese Americans or black marines are asked to leave the officer training program because they can't quite "cut it." The few who remain in the program are not promoted at the same rate as white colleagues. Ninety percent of all marine officers are white.

Nor are Asians singled out only in the Marines. They have currently become a major target for employment discrimination in general. Unfortunately, too many Americans tend to lump all Asians into one basket, no matter where they came from or when they or their families arrived here. Ironically, some of the worst recent cases of discrimination have occurred because of black or Hispanic actions against Asians who have achieved economic success. (Recent cases in point occurred in California, during the Los Angeles riots following the Rodney King trial, and on the East Coast, after the shooting of a black by a Korean grocery store owner.) It's a sad commentary on our society—the best democratic society in the world—that *the last into the United States seems to be the first discriminated against.*

One hundred and twenty-five years ago, it was the Irish who "need not apply" for jobs; then it was the Italians and Jews who were routinely picked up on New York's Lower East Side on a Saturday night so that if some crime went down, the police would already have likely suspects in jail. And now Asians have become the victims of choice.

In one case I am handling, June was the only female Chinese civilian employee in her department at a now-closed naval base. Two years before the base closed, in accordance with navy regulations, she filed an internal complaint of racial discrimination arising out of disciplinary action taken against her. She complained about being criticized for her performance (which had always been praised), and being singled out for being late or for using office time for personal business, when her non-Asian colleagues did the same routinely. When the case was reviewed, the navy investigator found in her favor, rescinded the disciplinary actions against her, and all negative letters were expunged from her personnel file. Not surprisingly, June's supervisors, who had disciplined her, were not happy.

Shortly afterward, when it was common knowledge there would be a downsizing at the base in the not-too-distant future, her supervisors began to deny June opportunities for advancement and, slowly but surely, reassigned all her duties to other employees. When the anticipated downsizing came, June was terminated because now, having no duties, her job was "superfluous." The case on her behalf, alleging "unlawful discrimination and retaliation," is now pending in federal court.

As indicated earlier, there seems to be a pecking order to discrimination, and unfortunately Hispanics have also had to pay unfair dues. In one case I represented Luis, who had been with a national charity for thirty-one years and held a key management position. The charity's stated severance policy was a minimum of one week's pay for every year of service. About two years ago, in a downsizing in which Luis was the only Hispanic laid off, he received far less severance than that given to short-term Caucasian workers who were discharged at the same time. Luis got the minimum, while some of his Caucasian counterparts received severance at the rate of several weeks' pay for each year of service. The charity came up with various "explanations," none of which held water.

Yet, inexplicably, a judge accepted these explanations and dismissed Luis's claim. As discussed later on, the judge's rationale might best be described as peculiar, but Luis's misfortune shows that sometimes (but not usually) even those cases that apparently have merit can be lost. One theory was that Luis's situation might be accounted for by the fact that his employer was a highly regarded charity which was given the benefit of the doubt for its "good work," particularly as Luis's case might be rationalized away as only involving severance pay rather than discharge.

Another case in which I represented an Hispanic employee, however, had a much happier ending. In fact, it did not even require a lawsuit. After I notified the company (which had a dismal record of failing to hire Hispanics) that fired Marlene (supposedly for unsatisfactory performance) of her intention to sue, the company promptly offered her a vastly improved severance package, plus an additional sum to defray her legal expenses. Marlene accepted, and the case was settled before it was even officially begun.

With all the current attention on affirmative action concerning minorities and women, questions of religious discrimination have had far less attention. Nonetheless, it is still an issue. The term "religious belief" is given a very broad definition by the courts. The critical factors are that while the particular belief need not fall within a universally held concept of religion, the employee's beliefs must be sincerely held and conform to the individual's concept of "religious."

Under the law, one's religious beliefs are accorded the same protection as one's age, race, sex, national origin, or disability. Thus, they may not be held up to ridicule in the workplace (nor, for that matter, *anyplace*). In a recent case, a Jewish woman employed at a world famous jewelry store finally had her day in court and won. After being fired in 1984, she filed charges of sexual harassment and religious discrimination against the company, stating that her supervisors mocked her by using Yiddish terminology and pseudo-Jewish accents. To read the court papers in this case is to find oneself back in what would seem to be the Dark Ages, but it brings home the fact that blatant anti-Semitism and other types of religious discrimination continue to exist. In any event, after the case was pending for ten long years at a state human rights agency, the jewelry store worker was finally awarded $365,000 in 1995.

Another case in the news last year involved a "twofer" victim, to use the term mentioned earlier. In mid-1995, a former news anchor for a major city television station filed a discrimination suit claiming her dismissal was the result of anti-Semitism and her age. In her suit, the TV journalist claimed that shortly after a replacement news director was hired, she was ousted from her anchor post with the "News at Noon," and then she was given assignments that conflicted with her observance of the Sabbath. Although her religious commitment was acknowledged in her employment contract with the station, where she had worked for sixteen years, little by little the religious accommodations made to her were eroded. The forty-three-year-old ex-anchor also charged that her age was a factor in her transfer from the high-profile job as anchor to less glamorous reporting assignments. When station executives asserted that other Jewish employees were not discriminated against, this newswoman said, "When someone commits a murder, you don't have to prove they murdered everyone else around them."

◆ ◆ ◆

PART TWO

The Why, What, and How of
Pursuing an Employment
Discrimination Claim

Chapter 6

How to Pursue a Claim of Employment Discrimination

Okay. You've read the preceding chapters and/or consulted with a lawyer or your local EEOC or state human rights office; and you believe you've been the victim of employment discrimination. So what now?

The first thing you must do to ensure that you will not waive (lose) your protection under the law is to file your charge of discrimination in a timely manner. That is, within the deadline established by law. Remember, if you fail to do so, it's all over.

When to File

To pursue a claim under one of the federal laws (Title VII and its various amendments, ADEA or ADA), you must file a charge within *180* days of the discriminatory act. If you live in a state that also has its own human rights agency, the time to file can be extended to *300* days. Seems simple enough, right? Maybe not. The clock starts running when you have clear, definite, unequivocal *notice* of the discriminatory act itself, not when it actually occurs. It is the day your boss tells you that you are being fired, *not* the last day you actually work. If both events happen on the same day, no problem. But if on the first of the month your boss gives you two weeks' notice that you will be terminated on the fifteenth, you must start counting from the first, not the fifteenth.

The issue is further clouded by what the law means by "clear, definite, and unequivocal" notice. I briefly alluded to the problem (in chapter 1) in our discussion of the metals trader who was first notified he was being terminated a full year before the firing actually took effect.

But I can give you an even better illustration of the potential mischief that can result from different interpretations of the phrase "clear, definite, and unequivocal" notice. One of my current clients, a fifty-six-year-old senior advertising account executive, had an employment contract with a company that owned a number of ad agencies. The contract provided that he could be terminated, so long as his employer gave him six months advance written notice.

The company assigned Mike to one of the subsidiary ad agencies it owned, where he worked for about a year. In July 1992, the president of the subsidiary notified Mike in writing that he would be discharged on January 20, 1993. The grounds: the ubiquitous "poor performance." Mike was upset because he knew his performance was far better than that of three much younger account execs who had not been fired. A couple of weeks later, the head of the parent company's human resources department called Mike, told him not to worry about the termination notice because they were a huge organization, and they would try to get him a position with another of the ad agencies they owned. And subsequently, interviews were arranged.

In early September, Mike was told he was the right guy for a major position at a prominent agency. He was assured that the job would be his. All that was necessary was for the head of that particular agency to "sign off" on his hiring—it was a "mere formality." Mike relaxed and waited . . . and waited for the final meeting. It never came. First, the head of the agency was out of the country on business. Then it was the holiday season. Mike was told not to worry, he was still on the payroll, and the agency head would get in touch with him. A little nervous, but not unduly concerned, Mike did as he was told. It was not until January 20, 1993, came and went that Mike fully understood that he had been fired. It came as a major shock that threw Mike into a state of depression. He didn't really focus on a possible age discrimination claim.

. Still without a new job, Mike waited almost six months before he consulted me in August 1993. Based upon his version of the relevant events, it looked as if he had a case. But Mike couldn't make up his mind whether to proceed with legal action. In late September, he decided to do so, and by early October, we had filed a charge of age discrimination with the EEOC. Importantly, this all took place in a state that had its own human rights agency, because it was now *almost fifteen months* after Mike had first been told that he would be fired; but it was only *280 days* after his last day on the payroll. After waiting the mandatory 60 days, we filed a lawsuit in federal court. Coming as no surprise to me, the company moved (asked) for a court order dismissing Mike's case because he had failed to file an agency discrimination charge within 300 days of the company's "clear, definite, and unequivocal" notice of termination.

We opposed the motion on two grounds: 1. The notice

of termination came from the subsidiary agency to which Mike had been assigned, not from the parent company with which Mike had his employment contract. 2. Regardless of how clear, definite, and unequivocal the notice had been, it was rendered *un*clear, *un*definite, and *very* equivocal by the subsequent actions of the company, which had led Mike to believe he was really being transferred rather than fired. Fortunately, the court agreed with us and refused to throw out Mike's case. Without deciding whether the company's actions were in good faith or a deliberate effort to mislead Mike, the court simply decided that the company had so undermined the clarity of the original notice that Mike should not be considered to have known for certain that he was being discharged until his last day on the payroll, January 20, and he had filed with the EEOC within 300 days of that date. Now the case will proceed.

What is the moral of Mike's case? First, carefully think through whether you want to sue for discrimination. But once you make up your mind to do so, don't delay. File that charge with the EEOC or your local state agency as soon as possible. When you compute your time to file, err on the side of the earliest possible date you could be considered as knowing you would suffer employment discrimination.

Where to File

Although we have touched earlier on the question of where to file your claim for employment discrimination, here again is the step-by-step procedure:

There are four different venues available to pursue a case of employment discrimination: EEOC, state or local agencies, state courts, or the federal United States District Court. If you select the state court, you can proceed directly with your suit. If you choose the federal court, you must first file with the EEOC or a state or local agency. For claims brought under Title VII or the ADA, you must file with the EEOC and then request from it a "Notice of Right to Sue" letter (informing you that the EEOC's involvement has ended and you have ninety days to file in federal court). Such notice is routinely granted upon request of the person who filed the charge after the charge has been pending for six months. Today, recognizing that it will not get a chance to review your claim within six months because of its massive backlog, the EEOC may be willing to waive the waiting period upon request and issue the "Right to Sue" letter much earlier than the six-month period.

To sue in federal court under the ADEA, you need only file a charge with the EEOC, wait sixty days, and then proceed directly to the U.S. District Court. Alternatively, you could file your age discrimination charge with a state agency. After sixty days you would then ask the agency to dismiss the agency claim and, upon receipt of notice that it had done so, file in federal court. If you choose this route, *be careful*. The basis upon which the state agency dismisses your charge is *critical*. Make sure that it does not do so on the merits (an evaluation of its legal sufficiency) or for jurisdictional reasons (whether it has the authority to rule on your charge). You should clearly request that your charge be dismissed for *the sole and exclusive purpose of allow-*

ing you to file suit in court. In some states this is called a dismissal for reasons of "administrative convenience."

As you can see, given a choice, which you do have, it is much simpler and less risky to file the age discrimination charge with the EEOC and proceed from there.

Obviously, if for financial or other reasons, you intend to allow either the EEOC or state agency to process your claim to conclusion, you need only file with either one or the other agency, and let it "do its thing."

Although you can't go from court back to an agency, should you change your mind (because of lengthy delays or for some other reason), you can proceed to court from the agency at any time until it decides your case. Or, if you have filed with the EEOC, you will have ninety days to file in court after the EEOC notifies you that it has completed all action it intends to take in your case.

How to File

If you are represented by a lawyer, you don't have to be concerned with the mechanics of filing a discrimination charge or lawsuit. Your attorney knows how and will take care of it. If, however, you elect to pursue your claim through the EEOC or state agency on your own, the first step is to file the charge of discrimination. The charge itself is a legal document that sets forth the basis of your claim. Both the EEOC and state agency have forms available. Both will also assist you in filling them out. So, look up the address and telephone number of your agency of choice (you can find these listings in your telephone directory under the heading for state or federal government).

Call for an appointment and then meet with one of their representatives. Bring any documents or other evidence with you that support your claim and be prepared to give as detailed an explanation of the basis of your claim as possible. Filing is essentially a simple process and will be aided by agency representatives.

This is a good time to give you a few words of warning about filing a claim for unemployment benefits. If your company has said that you were terminated for "performance," and you believe the real reason for your dismissal was discrimination, when you fill out your unemployment application, state *your* reason, *not* the company's. In following through on your discrimination claim, you will leave a paper trail—and it's important that this trail be consistent with your account of discrimination.

Many people believe that if they resign from a job, they cannot collect unemployment insurance or pursue a discrimination suit. *This can be a very costly mistake.* When a person resigns his position because his employer has created intolerable working conditions, the resignation may qualify as a "constructive discharge," which means that it is treated for legal purposes the same as if he had been fired.

Remember, in chapter 4, about disability discrimination, I told you Ted's story: When his company discovered he had leukemia, they cut back on his duties, and demoted him, which led him to resign. That was a classic case of constructive discharge. By demeaning and humiliating him, the company made it impossible for Ted to continue. So, legally, his leaving was regarded as if the company had just thrown him out the door.

How Will My Case Be Processed by the Agency?

Once you have filed your charge, a copy is sent to your employer or former employer, who is then asked to submit a written response. Some agencies leave it to the company as to how to frame its response; others send out specific requests for relevant information.

After each side has presented its respective position on the claim, the agency representative who is handling the case will probably hold one or more conferences with you and your employer, the purpose of which is to refine the evidence produced so that it can be better analyzed and also to explore possible settlement. At the EEOC, settlement (or conciliation, as the EEOC calls it) is the ultimate goal. Failing to get the parties to agree, in almost all cases (except the very rare instances where it will sue in federal court on your behalf), will terminate the EEOC's involvement. Because of its limited legal staff, the EEOC only takes on major landmark or class action cases, those cutting edge issues involving hundreds of people. The important thing to remember about the EEOC is that it doesn't have adjudicative authority. In other words, it can't make a binding decision in a case; it can investigate and attempt to settle via conciliation, but that's all.

Once it has decided it can do no more than facilitate settlement, it will send you the "Notice of Right to Sue" letter informing you that it is terminating its investigation of your claim and giving you ninety days to file a suit in federal court. Should you fail to do so, that will be the end of your case. The ball game is over.

If, on the other hand, you selected a state human rights

agency (which has procedures for actually *resolving* complaints of discrimination), the failure to achieve settlement will not automatically conclude the process. While procedures vary from state to state, agencies such as the New York State Division of Human Rights make a preliminary determination, based upon the evidence submitted and the conferences conducted, as to whether there is sufficient reason to believe the employer has violated the law. If so, it issues a Probable Cause Determination, which has the effect of placing the case on a calendar (waiting list) for an administrative hearing (which is like a trial).

At the hearing, held before an administrative law judge employed by the agency, you and your employer can introduce evidence and witnesses to prove, or disprove, your claim. Each of you is entitled to be represented by a lawyer (which the Division will supply to you, free of charge). After all the evidence is in, the administrative law judge issues a decision, which has the same legal effect as a court order or jury verdict. If either party is not satisfied, the decision can be appealed in New York, for example, to the Appelate Division of the supreme court, at which the decision will either be upheld or reversed.

Sounds good, right? Maybe. One reason many people with employment discrimination grievances don't go to state agencies—or ultimately give up on them—is that the processing takes forever because of the enormous workloads. We just talked about such a case, the estate jewelry expert fired from the elegant jewelry store in 1984. Ten years later she won an award of $365,000. So she triumphed. Yes . . . but it took *ten years* for the state agency to rule on the case.

Still, working with a state agency is a viable alternative

for people who can't afford to sue in court. Even though you may experience an inordinately long delay, you will be provided with a lawyer, and the case will eventually be heard.

After reviewing all your options, you may decide that you want a lawyer of *your* choice, handling your case. In Part Three, we'll discuss the various ramifications of finding and working with an attorney.

PART THREE

Common Concerns and Misconceptions About Filing a Lawsuit

Chapter 7

Myths and Misconceptions

> *Misconception*—An erroneous notion.
> *Myth*—A traditional or legendary story, usually concerning a super human being with or without a basis in fact . . . a collective belief that is built up in response to the wishes of the group instead of an analysis of what it pertains to.

Myths and misconceptions are common throughout our society, and the legal arena is no exception. To the ordinary person, the world of litigation is shrouded in mystery and folklore, as depicted in books, television, and the movies. The legal drama unfolds in imposing courtrooms presided over by judges sitting at elevated benches. The fate of litigants is decided by jurors who make their decision based on witness testimony and other evidence. Actors on shows like "L.A. Law" and "Law and Order" portray lawyers who are canny and persuasive. They are inevitably able to elicit confessions of misconduct from the highest and mightiest, as well as the most hardened villains. Litigants are articulate, glamorous, and well-to-do. It is a world foreign to most.

So where do John or Jane Q. American fit into the litigation picture when they believe they have suffered employment discrimination at the hands of a large—or even small—employer? For a discharged employee, the specter of bringing a lawsuit, particularly against a former employer, is intimidating and daunting. The reality of what is involved is often obscured by the myths and misconceptions that surround lawsuits against employers.

On the other hand, while employers generally are more sophisticated in the ways of litigation, they, too, can be influenced by the very same myths and misconceptions. The great risk for employers is that they may start to believe their own "press notices."

In employment discrimination litigation, the employer does not always wear devil's horns . . . and the employee does not always wear a halo. Many, if not most, employers do not unlawfully discriminate against their employees—they don't because it is *unlawful* to do so, because they are *well-intentioned,* or because it is simply *bad business.*

Nonetheless, employers can be, and are, targeted for employment discrimination actions brought in the good faith but sometimes mistaken belief that the employer has violated the law. As employers do not have an exclusive on wrongful motivation, employee lawsuits against them can also arise from a desire for revenge, to leverage a better severance pay package, or for other improper reasons. One plumbing supplies distributor, which I have represented for close to twenty years, "bends over backward" to insure a discrimination-free workplace. Nevertheless, it was recently the target of an obviously unwarranted age and disability discrimination claim by an employee who, after numerous "second chances," was finally fired for unsatisfactory performance. I fully expect this claim to be dismissed by the state civil rights agency for lack of merit. But

innocent or guilty, employers must take care to evaluate re-
alistically their situations. Just as myths and misconceptions
can act as a deterrent to *employee lawsuits,* they can also
create a false sense of security for an *employer faced with
legal action.*

Among the most common myths and misconceptions
confronting the parties to employment discrimination disputes are:

1. The belief that the employee cannot afford to retain a
    lawyer (chapter 8).

2. The image of the big, "deep pockets" employer as in-
    vincible (chapter 9).

3. The fear of blackballing or other employer retaliation
    (chapter 10).

4. The belief that the case will be tied up in the courts for
    years (chapter 11).

By and large, however, these are erroneous myths or misconceptions without any basis in fact.

Chapter 8

I Can't Afford a Lawyer

While there have been lawyers experienced in employment discrimination law since passage, more than twenty-five years ago, of the society-changing state and federal statutes prohibiting such actions, this field of practice enjoyed neither high visibility nor glamour status until recently.

During the roaring 1980s, the legal profession's attention was focused on more free-wheeling, trendy, high-profile endeavors, such as real estate, corporate takeovers, and the like. But times change, and lawyers are, if anything, an adaptable species. Today, more than ever before, a large pool of attorneys is available from which the would-be job-bias plaintiff can choose.

Currently, the heavy media coverage of class action age discrimination suits and charges of sex discrimination, sexual harassment, racial prejudice, and denial of the rights of the disabled has made lawyers as well as the general public aware of these claims and has contributed to the reason why more lawyers are practicing employment discrimination law.

How Can I Find a Sympathetic, Experienced Lawyer?

While it may not yet be a "buyer's market" for employees seeking to retain counsel, the prospective litigant can and should be selective in his or her choice. As with most things in life, prudence and research are recommended when selecting an attorney. Just as you would investigate a specialist in the medical profession before undergoing treatment or surgery, so should you be cautious in selecting a lawyer to represent you in a job discrimination action.

One proviso: family lawyers, like family doctors, may not be your best choice when your life or your livelihood is on the line. The family lawyer who has advised your family about property, wills, and the like may not be specialized enough to counsel you about job-related problems. He might, for example, have difficulty recognizing a case of employment discrimination and therefore, upon learning you didn't have an employment contract, suggest you take the severance package offered, count your blessings, and fold your tent. On the other hand, a good family lawyer, like a good family doctor, may be aware of his own limitations, while recognizing what's happening in the world "out there," and recommend that you find a specialist.

When you're looking for a legal expert in employment discrimination, you can learn about his or her background, experience, and qualifications by talking to other lawyers, the local bar association, or via word of mouth among friends and associates. In any community, whether it's New York City, or Seattle, or Indianapolis, the legal fraternity is relatively small, and it should take only a few phone calls to discover the reputation and credentials of a would-be counsel. For the employee who is considering filing a case, this provides confidence in his choice; once a choice has been made, and the employer has been served with papers starting a lawsuit, those same few phone calls made by the *employer* checking out his opposition can provide a real impetus for a favorable settlement, when the employee's lawyer has a successful record in litigating such cases.

Often newspaper or TV reports of current cases in your area can yield the name of legal specialists who are willing to consult with you . . . or take on your cause. Consumer advocacy groups, such as NOW, ACLU, NAACP, and LAMBDA, provide lists of lawyers with specific expertise and may have attorneys available who are willing to take on *pro bono* (no fee) cases.

Hiring a lawyer, however, should involve more than a consideration of fees that will be charged. Litigation can be a personal and emotional experience, and the best relationship is one in which the employee feels comfortable with his attorney. Some people prefer a hard-driving, nononsense type, while others may want a more compassionate, comforting person. Whichever style is preferred, the relationship between counsel and client should work as smoothly as the proverbial "hand in glove."

This is, of course, a two-way street. I, and most lawyers involved in job bias suits, want to feel confident about the case we're about to take on. This is the most litigious society in the world, and too many people are quick to say "I'll sue." But that's not what most of us look for; we want to bring lawsuits that make sense for those plaintiffs we feel have a good chance of winning. That's not simply because if we win for the plaintiff, we can earn decent fees, but more important morally, with an employment discrimination case, the client is frequently unemployed, and the last thing he or she needs, when already experiencing financial hardship, is to commit to a case that has little chance of a favorable outcome.

Personally, when initially evaluating a case, I rely greatly on my own intuitive feel about the person involved. In addition to my obvious concern about the legal elements of the case, I want to know if he or she is sincere. Does his or her story make sense? Are there some great gaps in the recounting of the situation that may come back to haunt me as we proceed to trial? Remember, many cases turn on one person's word against another's. At the onset, I like to feel confident about *my person's* credibility (truthfulness/believability).

An attorney consulted for the first time by a prospective plaintiff faces two powerful incentives to assess fully and accurately the merits of the claim. The first is the attorney's ethical obligation to give the best advice possible. The second is the attorney's own stake in taking on a case in which the likelihood of being compensated is directly related to the prospects of either winning at trial or of reaching a settlement with the former employer. The last thing an attorney wants or needs is to take on a "loser"—a case that, despite even heroic efforts, will not succeed and, consequently, will fail to bring in any revenue.

It is important for the attorney to evaluate a case properly because once taken on, it must be seen through to conclusion. Generally, a lawyer can only drop a case with the court's permission, and courts are reluctant to grant this because it can leave a client unrepresented right in the middle of a case. Undoubtedly, the net effect of these considerations is that employee attorneys are more conservative about accepting cases than are *employers'* attorneys who, by doing so, have virtually nothing to lose, as discussed in the next chapter.

What Financial Options Do I Have?

Litigation in general, and an employment discrimination suit in particular, is generally an expensive process. Just how expensive depends upon numerous variables: the complexity of the case, prevailing hourly rates for lawyers and supporting services, litigation philosophy of the defense/employer's attorneys (are they cooperative and conciliatory *or* combative and confrontational?), and whether the case is settled or carries all the way through to trial and even appeal.

If fees are calculated on hourly rates, it is not at all uncommon for legal fees in a suit *proceeding through trial* to be in the $50,000 to $100,000 realm per party, so total legal fees (for both parties) generated in a single lawsuit may be double that amount. This combined cost is particularly important for *employers* because they can be required to pay a successful employee's legal fees as well as their own.

Most employee attorneys recognize that high five-figure fees are virtually impossible for the ordinary person, particularly if unemployed. Therefore, other types of fee arrangements are not unusual. While some attorneys representing individuals still work only on an hourly fee basis, a contingent fee arrangement or a combination of minimum hourly fee and contingent fee is more common. With a contingency fee the attorney receives a percentage (perhaps 33 percent) of any recovery, either after trial or upon settlement. If the suit does *not* succeed, the attorney receives no fee. A contingency fee is the *equalizer,* allowing those who otherwise would be unable to afford an attorney to obtain legal representation.

To avoid the prospect of expending large amounts of time without any compensation, some lawyers work on a hybrid arrangement in which they are compensated for their time at an agreed-upon rate up to a maximum amount (perhaps $5,000 to $10,000), with the balance to be a contingency fee. This not only addresses the attorney's concern but also has the advantage of limiting the fees paid by the employee. For example, it might be agreed between you and your counsel that he will bill for his time at the rate of $200 per hour for each hour of service to a maximum of twenty-five hours, which would total $5,000. Once you pay this amount, no further payments are due, no matter how many hours your attorney subsequently commits to the case.

Upon a successful conclusion of the case (either through a court or jury verdict or settlement), to avoid double payment, the $5,000 will usually be applied toward any contingency fee due your lawyer. So, if the case is eventually won or settled for $150,000, the contingency fee would be $50,000 ($45,000 plus the $5,000 already paid).

But what about the person who cannot afford *any fee arrangement?* When any fee at all is too great a fee, there are options available, as discussed in chapter 6, for proceeding through a state or federal antidiscrimination agency, at which lawyers either are not necessary or are provided free of charge.

What About Other Expenses?

In addition to lawyer's fees, there are other costs of maintaining a lawsuit, including:

- ◆ **Court filing fees.** Perhaps $120 to $250
- ◆ **Witness fees.** Ranging from $40 for fact witnesses (those with knowledge of relevent events) to $2,000 to $4,000 per day for expert witness testimony, such as psychiatrists or psychologists who can describe the emotional distress an employee suffers when terminated, or statistical experts who can establish a pattern of discrimination against a particular protected class (i.e., females, disabled workers, or older persons) based on an analysis of hiring and firing practices.
- ◆ **Postage, copying, and process service fees.**
- ◆ **Deposition transcripts, which can represent the largest expense of litigation.** A deposition is a pretrial oral examination in which a witness or opposing party is questioned by the lawyers about his knowledge of, or involvement in, the lawsuit—in effect, it provides a preview of trial testimony and permits each party to learn the evidence the other side will present during a trial. The taking of depositions gives all parties the opportunity to evaluate the merits of the case for purposes of settlement, and/or to streamline the presentation of evidence at trial.

Unfortunately, given the propensity of reporting companies to employ a format of wide margins and quadruple spacing, the written (typed) transcripts of the oral depositions—which range from $3 to $6 per page—can get expensive. How expensive depends on the number of depositions taken and the length of each. But these costs can't be avoided or circumvented, since depositions are essential to the preparation of any case.

Who pays these costs, attorney or client, is a matter for negotiation. Sometimes the employee agrees to, and sometimes the attorney will advance the necessary amounts. Ideally, it becomes only a matter of advancing payment, as a prevailing (winning) employee is usually reimbursed "off the top" for expenses out of the settlement payment or jury award.

If I Sue and Lose, What Will It Cost?

I want to stress this point: Much of the impact on employees of legal fees and costs of federal court litigation has been dramatically reduced by judicial decisions providing that an employee who prevails on *any* of his discrimination claims at trial is entitled to an award of legal fees from his former employer. *The company is not accorded a similar right.* Even if an employer is totally successful in defending an employment discrimination suit, *it will not be entitled to a reimbursement of legal fees from the former employee.*

Providing specifically for an award of legal fees is unusual, even in our superlitigious society. To appreciate the significance of awarding legal fees to winning employees, consider what would happen if the American judicial system provided across the board for the losing party to pay the victor's legal fees *and* the costs of the lawsuit. Such a provision would just about eliminate lawsuits, much as it has in Canada. Most would-be litigants would be unwilling to take the risk of bringing a losing case.

For a long time, the federal courts were reluctant to

make legal fee awards in amounts approximating the true fees incurred by the successful job discrimination attorney, but this resistance has sharply dissipated in recent years. Federal courts now generally award an employee's lawyer, who wins his case at trial, fees approaching those actually incurred, provided they are based on a reasonable calculation. Courts expect the fees to be reasonable in terms of the hourly rate charged by the attorney, as compared to the rate of similarly experienced counsel in his locale and reasonable in terms of the number of hours expended for the services rendered. The change in attitude by the courts not only reduces the likelihood that an employee will ultimately bear the costs of litigation but also serves to motivate attorneys to represent employees.

While some state laws may also provide for payment of legal fees to a successful employee, the practice is by no means uniform, and undoubtedly is a prime reason why the majority of discrimination cases are brought in federal rather than state courts.

What this all boils down to is that in today's climate, any employee who believes that he or she has been the victim of job-related discrimination should not be prevented or deterred from pursuing a claim because of a perceived inability to afford a lawyer. By the same token, it makes it clear that no employer can take false comfort in the myth of lawyer unavailability, or believe that the ex-employee will not be able to afford or obtain competent legal representation because of a lack of finances.

◆ ◆ ◆

Chapter 9

I Can't Win Against My Deep-Pockets Employer

Lurking at the edges of each party's ultimate decision about how to handle a case are the ever-present myths and misconceptions surrounding the opposing party's chances of winning. The misconception that employers work hardest to foster and perpetuate is that of *employer invincibility*. How, workplace folklore posits, can a mere discharged employee with limited resources hope to defeat the large corporation, with its seemingly unlimited legal and financial capabilities? Fear of employer invincibility is cited most frequently as the reason for *not* pursuing an employment discrimination claim. *Incredibly, it is probably the greatest of all misconceptions.*

Before even addressing the relative likelihood that one party or the other will prevail in a job bias case, the threshold question must be whether the claim should even be brought by the employee, and if so, whether it should be vigorously resisted by the employer. At least in theory, the first and most efficient screening out of cases is done by the legal profession itself. Because of the risk, cost, and time involved, the initial advice of lawyers to clients and/or prospective clients is critical, and should head off much needless litigation.

The decision-making process for employer attorneys is

less acute than that of employee attorneys, as discussed earlier in chapter 8. Although they operate at the same disadvantage of receiving a potentially slanted portrayal of events from their prospective client, they are not confronted with the same financial dilemma. Corporate attorneys are almost always retained on an hourly basis and, therefore, have no reason to decline a case because no matter what the outcome, they will be handsomely compensated as they do their legal and factual research to determine the validity of their client's position. Unlike the employee's attorneys, who must evaluate a case without benefit of familiarity with the company's defenses, the corporate attorneys have the luxury of postponing a *final* assessment until the discovery phase of the case has been completed. While the employer will certainly incur defense costs during discovery, which are a deterrent to frivolous defenses, neither he nor his attorney is irrevocably committed to going all the way until pretty late in the game. An incidental advantage to employers is that employees often find this waiting game frustrating, and sometimes even frightening.

On the other hand, it is well known to companies and their lawyers that we are a nation that favors the underdog—and juries don't like to see an injured party go away empty-handed. In that vein, the consensus is that more verdicts favor employees than employers.

A glaring illustration of this phenomenon is found in a case I handled back in the days (six years ago) when I was exclusively a management labor lawyer. A sixty-one-year-old magazine advertising salesman for a large publisher, who had been employed there for about seven years, for some unknown reason took it upon himself to disregard well-established procedures for making sales calls on accounts. Rather than going through the advertising/marketing departments of the companies on which he called, he reportedly began barging in on senior executives, even the presidents, of top *Fortune* 500 companies. Three of these companies told the salesman's boss (the publisher of his magazine) that they considered the salesman persona non grata, and he was prohibited from making further calls on their staffs.

Since these three advertisers were the source of most of the business generated by the salesman, there appeared to be substantial grounds for firing him. However, my client (the magazine) elected instead to transfer the salesman to a new territory and give him a fresh start. In less than four months, three of the major accounts in the new territory voiced similar complaints about the salesman and again barred him from their premises. The magazine now had had enough. He was fired.

I was very surprised when the salesman filed an age discrimination suit against the magazine. I saw no way he could win. I was so sure about it that I would have gone double or nothing on my usual fee. In fact, I may even have made that suggestion to my client. If I did, the client was equally confident of victory and rejected the proposal.

In any event, when it came time for trial, I did not rely solely on the publisher of the magazine to tell the jury why he had fired the salesman. At the company's expense, we also flew in five of the six marketing executives who had refused to deal with the salesman (the sixth provided a sworn deposition, which was read to the jury). Under oath, each described in detail for the jury the salesman's behavior, which had led to their demands that he be taken off their accounts. I saw our case as overwhelming and incontrovertible, especially as the salesman's case was comprised of nothing more than his personal belief that his age was the motivating factor in his discharge.

While the jury was deliberating, I expressed my opinion that *my* case was a sure winner to the salesman's lawyer, whom I had known for some years. He just looked at me, winked, and said, "Yeah, but my guy cried on the witness stand." It was true, he had, but I dismissed this as amateurish theatrics. Even the judge had looked at him incredulously and asked, "What are you crying about?"

Anyway, it took the jury just one hour to award the salesman everything he had asked for: back pay, emotional distress damages, and even several years front (future) pay. To me, the message was clear.

As a footnote, we appealed the decision and were successful in vacating the front pay award. The rest of the verdict was allowed to stand.

Employers are well aware of this jury disposition. But what is not widely known is *why* the general attitude of juries does not serve as a greater deterrent to discriminatory actions by employers. One reason, of course, is the lack of a proper understanding or appreciation for the merits of the lawsuit. This can happen when top management executives who will be called upon to defend suits really know nothing about them. Remember, discrimination does not require the involvement or prior knowledge of top management. An employer, corporate or otherwise, is responsible for the acts of its managers, supervisors, and agents, acts that it cannot always control. Thus, employers can be held liable for ageism, sexism, or racism that they might, with prior knowledge, have avoided.

But after giving senior executives the benefit of a doubt for being unwilling participants in some suits, in other situations their role can be far more insidious. Employers have been known to make a conscious decision to absorb the financial repercussions of discrimination because it is a "cost-effective" method of doing business. An example would be an employer who wishes to lower costs by reducing the number of older, higher paid members of its staff—in other words, downsizing.

So this is a not-so-rare occurrence: a company selects older workers for discharge in the belief that a younger staff will be more energetic and command lower salaries. The employer may conclude that when the smoke has cleared, it will have gained a financial advantage of having a younger, less costly workforce. In the long run, the short-term impact of defending, settling, or losing age discrimination suits may be more than offset.

Here's a hypothetical example based on one of my cases. A medium-size marketing company, looking to boost its profits, zeroed in on nine executives in their late forties and fifties, who individually earned from $60,000 to $110,000 a year, for an aggregate total of $800,000 annually, plus medical insurance, pension contributions, and life insurance premiums, which represented another $200,000 to $300,000. In a typical downsizing/rightsizing move, the company fired all nine employees, paying severance packages totaling about $400,000.

But in the long run, by replacing them with *five younger employees,* whose salaries averaged $50,000 a year, for a total of $250,000, even considering medical insurance, other benefits, and perks, the company saved hundreds of thousands of dollars annually. The employer took a risk that none of the fired executives would sue. Only one did, and it cost the company a settlement of $300,000 . . . small potatoes when you consider what it would save over the next ten years.

The same rationale can be applied to getting rid of disabled workers, or women who take time off for childbirth, or employees who seek leaves to care for ill family members, or to any other employees deemed financially expendable. Therefore, even in the face of legal prejudice, in today's world, employers may believe from a dollars-and-cents viewpoint that employment discrimination can be good business. If this is so, the only way to take the profit out of workplace discrimination is for more employees to pursue legal action and for courts and juries to impose the maximum cost on guilty employers.

Experience reveals (and employers know) that, of any group of persons discriminatorily discharged, a certain number *will not sue,* either because they elect to retire, find other employment, or are deterred by the myths and misconceptions we've been talking about. Of those who do file a claim, some may lose heart and abandon their suit along the way, and some employees may even lose their cases for any number of reasons. However, in the absence of statistics available to the public, it is generally estimated that some 80 percent of employment discrimination claims are settled out of court. Because any payment by the employer to settle a case is more than the employee would have received had he simply accepted his fate and not taken up the fight, a settlement represents a victory for the worker.

The size of the settlement simply indicates the extent of the victory.

Let's face it, in some instances, employers can win just by overwhelming the other side. They are so big they can be intimidating—but if the plaintiff and his lawyer are willing to "hang tough," not be intimidated, and stick it out to the end, the prospects are bright. Here's an example of one of my cases, where a particularly brutal and heavy-handed major conglomerate thought its sheer clout and legal staff grandeur could overwhelm a plaintiff's case.

A woman, let's call her Betty, who had been administrative assistant to a high-ranking honcho of the company, had been sexually harassed by another executive. When she complained to her boss, she was told—amazingly—that she should *apologize* for filing a complaint against the fine gentleman who had harassed her. Then Betty became ill, and although she continued to work, she was denied a promotion, she thought, because of her prior sexual harassment complaint and her illness. Betty filed an internal complaint in accordance with company policy encouraging "in house" resolution of discrimination claims and was immediately *demoted* to a position where the environment had the potential of worsening her illness.

When she sued for the retaliatory demotion, she was promptly fired. Betty's suit sought money damages for several causes of action: sexual harassment, denial of promotion, violation of the ADA, and retaliatory demotion and discharge. Also included was a multimillion-dollar claim for emotional distress and punitive damages for the employer's conduct, which included spying on her during the lawsuit and digging into her personal and professional background.

The conglomerate brought its heavy legal guns into the fray, spearheaded by a *female attorney* who, it felt, would make a better impression on the judge or jury than a rough, tough male "beating up on" poor defenseless Betty. The legal team took numerous depositions, most of them unnecessary and dealing with testimony inadmissable in court, at a cost of thousands and thousands of dollars. These tactics prolonged discovery far longer than necessary. Next the legal staff made the de rigueur motion for "summary judgment," requesting that the judge dismiss the case on the grounds that there was not sufficient evidence to even send it to the jury. As we said earlier, employers' lawyers have nothing to lose by such a motion because in the final analysis, even if they lose, the company will be in no worse a position than had it not made the motion in the first place, and it places the burden of defending against the motion on the plaintiff.

Still, Betty did what she had to do. Frightened and intimidated as she was, she stood her ground. Then, because even this huge, deep-pockets employer was feeling the pinch of the enormous legal expenses it was incurring, and because it was finally coming to the realization that Betty would not be cowed and would see it through to the end, not to mention its distaste for the widespread negative publicity the case was engendering, the employer suggested settlement, and the case was settled.

The point of this chapter is to lay to rest the myth of *employer invincibility*. Will your former company bring out the big legal guns? *Yes*. Will it try to itimidate you? *Probably*. Will this artillery blast your chances for a fair trial or settlement? *No*. Will the tactics of fear and intimidation succeed? *Not unless you allow them to*. Federal and state laws are on *your* side if you have a valid case of discrimination. Aside from the law, your major strength is having solid, knowledgeable, dedicated, and determined legal representation. Sure, employee v. employer is a case of David v. Goliath. But remember who won that lopsided battle.

Chapter 10

My Employer Will Retaliate
I Will Be Blackballed

Ranking third after the myths and misconceptions that an employee may not be able to afford an attorney or that he will have to play the role of David taking on the formidable Goliath-employer is the misguided notion—based on fear—that any employee who sues his employer for discrimination will automatically suffer retaliation or be "blackballed" and jeopardize chances for future employment.

Retaliating in any fashion against a current employee for availing himself of his rights under federal antidiscrimination laws is specifically forbidden by Title VII, as well as a series of major court decisions. If you do nothing more than file a discrimination charge or bring a lawsuit, any adverse action taken against you by your employer solely because you did so is *illegal*.

This is a very sensitive area for those employers on the receiving end of a discrimination claim. No one likes being sued, including employers. A common first reaction is the desire to fire the "offender." However, if the employer is smart enough, or lucky enough, to consult his attorney before taking any rash action, he will almost certainly be told to "cool it" because all he will be doing is buying further legal action in the form of a claim for "unlawful retaliatory discharge." In fact, the most common advice in such circumstances is for the employer to "walk on eggshells" where the suing employee is concerned. In most cases, filing a discrimination claim is like buying an insurance policy against being fired.

This, however, does not mean that your employer will not try for revenge in some other way. For example, companies have sought to transfer suing employees to other jobs or restrict their access to confidential or sensitive information because of perceived disloyalty or conflict of interest. However, most courts have concluded that the mere filing of a discrimination claim, in and of itself, is not evidence of either. Something more is required, such as making disparaging remarks about the employer or encouraging other employees to file suit.

So, if you have occasion to charge your employer with some form of employment discrimination, be sure to "keep your nose clean." Do your job, don't be late to work, don't bad-mouth your boss or in any other way give the company an excuse to fire you, and you should be okay. But even if you take all these precautions, you might still be unlucky enough to have an employer who will take a shot at making your life on the job unpleasant in the hope that you will elect to quit.

My client Bill provides a good example. Bill was the second-ranking human resources manager at the same national charity that stiffed Luis by not giving him severance pay equal to that given his nonminority colleagues. Bill felt he had been denied promotion to the top position in his department in favor of a younger, less-experienced female employee because of his age (fifty-eight) and his history of heart disease. He brought suit against the charity for vio-

lating both the ADEA and the ADA. Soon afterward, he
was told that he now needed his new boss's permission to
access employee records or consult with colleagues concerning situations in which there was a possibility of an employment discrimination charge being filed by an employee
of the charity. He was also denied his annual performance
appraisal, according to the charity, because of a fear that
anything negative said about him might be cause for a
claim of retaliation.

Of course, we added a claim for unlawful retaliation to
Bill's suit. Bill's supervisors admitted that the charity had
no reason to suspect disloyalty, that Bill's performance and
behavior after filing the suit were perfectly acceptable, and
that the restrictions were motivated exclusively by the suit
itself and nothing more. In response to Bill's motion for
summary judgment on his claim of retaliation, the court
agreed that the charity's actions were illegal and directed
it to remove the restrictions and grant Bill his long-delayed
performance appraisal. This was done, and Bill is now
awaiting trial on his discriminatory denial of promotion
claim.

The problem for persons who have been *discharged* and
sue their former employer is somewhat different, although
also cloaked in the protection of the law.

Unfortunately, blackballing existed to some extent in
the past, especially in industries where "everybody knows
everybody" and may, to a rather limited degree, continue
at present. Generally speaking, however, today *blackballing
is bad business*. The legal consequences for the employer
far outweigh any benefit.

Probably the greatest deterrent to blackballing is our
country's laws against defamation (libel and slander). False

statements maliciously made about a man or woman that cause damage to that person, particularly in their employment capacity, are defamatory and actionable at law. A number of court decisions several years ago established that negative job references that were false could qualify as *slander,* if made verbally, or *libel,* if stated in writing.

Because giving a bad, false reference opens an employer to the possibility of a lawsuit for defamation, most former employers now respond to requests for employee references by supplying only "name, rank, and serial number." In other words, usually only a former worker's job title and dates of employment are supplied. By so doing, an employer protects itself against lawsuits. It would be difficult to find a sound business reason to go beyond such a policy, especially when an employer may already be the target of a discrimination case.

Keep in mind, too, most employers are well-intentioned and fair-minded. They do not subscribe to discriminatory practices and do not feel obliged to help another employer who has demonstrated job bias. Why take on someone else's problem? In most cases, there is no good reason morally or professionally . . . and they would be abetting an unlawful practice if they paid any attention to negative aspersions about you made by your former employer.

Legalities aside, can an employer really "stick it" to a former employee by giving negative appraisals to a prospective employer on the sly? It would be naive to rule it out. But is it worth it in practical business terms? The answer in most cases will be no. So, while the risk of blackballing will never be entirely eliminated, it is probably pretty small.

One of my clients, who has a very strong age discrimination suit against her former company, brought up the possibility of having a tainted reputation in her field—public relations. She was worried that her ex-boss might say she drank too much, since on occasion she might have two margaritas during business lunches. "Isn't it common in public relations to have a drink or two while doing business at lunch?" I asked, more rhetorically than not. She said it was. "Do the executives at your company have a couple of drinks when they go out to lunch?" "Of course—sometimes more than a couple." I assured her there was little to fear—aside from any legalities, it would be a question of the pot calling the kettle black.

In the final analysis, for many employees, fear of blackballing may have become a nonissue. Given today's difficult job market, fewer and fewer employees are able or willing to shrug off valid discrimination claims, especially when faced with reduced opportunities and fierce competition in finding a new, or equivalent, job.

Concern about the relatively slim possibility of being blackballed fades very quickly when the specter of bleak job prospects and a disastrous financial future faces them. Another point to consider, too, is that if there are strong grounds for a discrimination claim, and an ex-employee can prove he or she has been blackballed, that's one more actionable cause the worker can pursue and fight legally.

Chapter 11

My Case Will Be Tied up in Court for Years

As discussed earlier, there are several ways to pursue a claim of employment discrimination, through state or federal agencies or through state or federal courts. The duration of the process varies according to the forum chosen.

The speediest path to resolution lies in the federal courts. However, the amount of time it takes to see a case through to completion varies tremendously, depending on such factors as the volume of cases pending on the calendars of the various United States district courts. This volume is in turn dependent on the geographic location and the number of judges assigned to each district. Surprisingly, though, even in the Southern District of New York, which encompasses parts of New York City and its northern suburbs, a case can go from inception through trial in *as few as seven months*. This processing time would be unusually fast, though. More representative would be a period of twelve to twenty-four months.

If there is a settlement, the time will be shorter; appeals will extend the time.

State courts tend to be somewhat slower yet are frequently still in the range of eighteen to thirty months. State antidiscrimination agencies, whose services are free to those without lawyers, are overburdened with an increasing backlog of cases and usually require far longer time periods before a case is litigated. The state agencies also operate under staff reductions brought about by increasing fiscal restraints on the state itself. At the New York State Division of Human Rights, it can take up to five years to reach a trial or public hearing, as it is called. State agencies attempt to deal with their overwhelming caseload by actively seeking settlements. Cases successfully settled will naturally require less time.

Since the EEOC does not provide a mechanism to adjudicate (decide by trial) claims of discrimination, it can only seek to conciliate (settle) disputes or, in rare instances, file a federal lawsuit on behalf of an aggrieved individual or a class action claim for a group of individuals. If the EEOC is unable to settle a claim and is not willing to file suit, it can, in the final analysis, only refer the claimant to the federal courts. Therefore, if it settles a claim, the EEOC may be the quickest route to resolution, but failing to do so, the time spent there may bring the claimant no closer to a final disposition and could wind up being the slowest of the alternatives.

As discussed in chapter 6, the choice of forum, however, is not always clear-cut. In actual practice, a claim of employment discrimination may work its way through a combination of the different alternatives.

Remember Mary, the national sales manager for the major outerwear manufacturer discussed in chapter 2 who was fired on the day she was to start maternity leave? The discharge took place in mid-November 1988. In order to meet the prerequisite for bringing a sex/pregnancy discrimination case in federal court, she filed a charge with the

EEOC shortly after her termination. A few weeks later, she consulted with me, and after hearing her story, I agreed to represent her in a federal court suit on an hourly/contingency fee basis, with a maximum total hourly fee of $10,000. Mary decided not to go ahead with the federal court suit, electing instead to pursue her case through the EEOC on her own, without an attorney.

Because she had been employed in New York state, which has its own human rights agency, the EEOC deferred processing the charge to the state agency, where it languished for *four years*. Then, in late 1992, frustrated with the delay, Mary met with me again and retained me to file a federal court action on her behalf. During the next ten months, both sides engaged in a full discovery process, including interrogatories, document production requests, and several depositions.

By the end of 1993, one year after the suit was filed in the U.S. District Court, the case was settled. Although, under the terms of settlement, it is not possible to reveal the exact settlement figures, Mary was very satisfied with the outcome.

In addition to the time requirements of the court or agency, the speed with which a case works its way through the legal process is significantly affected by other variables, such as lawyers' schedules, their good faith efforts at moving the process forward, or, conversely, efforts at delay. Busy lawyers have to assign priorities among the matters they are handling, which can advance or retard the progress of a given case. While employees and their lawyers have a vested interest in moving a case toward trial, *employers and their lawyers do not*. Delaying the day of reckoning can put additional financial and psychological pressure on an employee; employers, who have nothing to gain and everything to lose at trial, have been known to resort to this tactic.

While it is clear that resolution of employment discrimination claims will not happen overnight, the time required is, by and large, tolerable, particularly when the only alternative is to forgo the process itself. And as I said before, staying the course to the end *vastly increases the employee's chances of a favorable outcome!*

PART FOUR

The Process: From Filing to Finale

Chapter 12

Let the Games Begin

Maybe this chapter should be called "The Beginning of the End," but that sounds ominous. What I'm about to describe has a much more upbeat goal: exactly what happens to you, the plaintiff, after you've satisfied your agency requirements (as described in chapter 6) and initiated a lawsuit for employment discrimination.

Lawsuits are commenced by filing a Complaint with the court and serving a copy on your adversary. The Complaint, which in skeletal form outlines the factual and legal basis for your claim, is not dissimilar to your agency charge of discrimination. You are called the plaintiff (the party that is suing). Service of the Complaint triggers the obligation on the part of your employer, who is the defendant (the party being sued), to file an Answer, which either admits or denies each allegation in your Complaint. These documents (Complaint and Answer) serve as the framework for the lawsuit.

The next stage is called Discovery. This is the process by which each side, following the procedural rules of the court, can and does obtain the evidence the other party expects to use to support, or defend against, the claim of discrimination. The process of Discovery is completed through the use of *interrogatories* (written questions that must be answered in writing by the other side), *document production requests* (requiring the other party to turn over pertinent written materials), and *depositions* (the process whereby one party's attorney questions the other party and witnesses who must respond under oath). *Discovery is the most extensive and most critical part of the process.* If the lawyers do their jobs properly, both you and your employer will know the other's case inside and out. The trial, when it comes, will just be the stage on which each side acts it out (through lawyers and witnesses) for the jury.

But at the end of Discovery, and before trial, you and the company each have the right to make *"dispositive"* motions before the judge. Dispositive motions (requests) are those that have the capability of terminating the case in favor of one party or the other. By far the motion most often used is the motion for summary judgment (which can be made by employers and employees alike), which I have mentioned earlier. To properly understand such a motion, you must keep in mind the basic tenet of litigation: questions of fact are to be resolved by the jury and questions of law by the judge. Therefore, except in those instances (now quite rare in employment discrimination cases) where the case is being handled by a judge without a jury, if there are disputed factual issues, the case must go to trial before a jury. It is only when the pertinent facts that underlie the claim of discrimination are not disputed by the parties, that a judge may apply the applicable law to these facts and decide the case.

As you must surely recognize by now, in employment discrimination cases the material (pertinent) facts are almost always in dispute. Is the reason the employer gives for the action it took against its employee the real reason, or is it in fact only a concocted excuse for discriminating against an employee because he or she was too old or a minority or a woman, etc. The courts have held that when questions of motive or intent are involved, summary judgment is usually inappropriate. Therefore, in employment discrimination cases, summary judgment motions do not succeed very frequently.

Employers know this but routinely seek summary judgment anyway. They have nothing to lose because losing the motion is no worse than not making it in the first place, and sometimes the employer might get lucky and win one. After all, there are instances in which an employee's case is so weak it should be dismissed. Another reason employers pursue summary judgment is the psychological effect it has on the employee, creating as it does the fear of defeat before even having his day in court, not to mention the additional financial costs it imposes on the employee whose attorney will have to file papers opposing the motion.

On the other hand, recognizing that a determination of whether the company's alleged "reason" for its actions is true or false will almost always be a disputed factual issue for the jury to resolve, employees rarely seek summary judgment, especially since they rarely have the financial resources to take a "flier." One of the exceptions to this "rule" is the case I discussed earlier involving Sarah, the government agency manager fired when she sought a reasonable accommodation under the ADA for her bursitis, which was aggravated by the mistreatment of her boss. In her case, both parties filed for summary judgment. The nature of her disability was not disputed, the questions were legal, not factual—whether her condition qualified as a disability under the ADA and whether the accommodation (transfer) she sought was reasonable under the ADA. It also was undisputed that she was still on a company-authorized medical leave (requiring that she be disabled from doing her job) at the time she was fired by the agency, which had failed to obtain its own doctor's approval of the discharge.

Because the essential facts were not in dispute, it made sense for the parties to seek this "shortcut" resolution to the dispute. However, even if Sarah prevails on her motion for summary judgment, the question of back pay, compensatory damages, and punitive damages will still have to be decided by a jury. To the extent that the jury will need to hear evidence of what the agency did to Sarah in order to set the amount of money to award for emotional distress and as punitive damages, the nature and extent of the evidence offered at trial may in the final analysis be minimally affected by granting summary judgment. Importantly, though, the question for the jury would no longer be whether my client would win but simply how much.

Trial, of course, is the objective of all plaintiffs. *The trial* represents their day in court . . . the chance to enforce rights made available by law. Unless one party or the other appeals the jury's verdict (which, as a general rule, is difficult to alter), this is the battlefield where the final and binding resolution of your employment discrimination claim is made.

I don't mean to suggest, however, that appeals are never appropriate or that they can only be taken from jury verdicts. A grant of summary judgment is also appealable. Remember Luis, the budget director for a national charity who was denied severance pay equivalent to that given his

Caucasian counterparts? The judge had initially granted summary judgment in favor of the charity, on the basis that since the employer had treated him well during his thirty-one-year career, it was "highly implausible" that it would discriminate against him at *the end of his career.*

Our first basis for appeal was that the judge had ignored the fact that top management at the charity had changed completely only three years before the discriminatory denial of severance pay, so there was no basis to bestow on the new bosses credit for the fair and unbiased behavior of their predecessors. Second, we argued that if allowed to stand, such a decision would give carte blanche to employers who had not previously discriminated against long-term employees to do so at the end of their careers without fear of punishment. It would also essentially remove severance pay from coverage of the antidiscrimination laws.

The court of appeals surprisingly ruled in favor of the charity (the "good works" factor again?) by accepting the charity's version of disputed facts. But, in its written opinion, the court made no reference at all to the "implausibility" of discrimination simply because it involved a question of the adequacy of severance pay at the end of a long and successful career.

And because when dealing with the legal process one must always be prepared for the unexpected, there is one last wrinkle in the process that is worth looking at. Filing a lawsuit in federal court is no guarantee that the court will ultimately decide your claim. Take the case of Andy, a sixty-two-year-old manager at a major insurance carrier. The previous year he had been transferred to a new boss. On Andy's sixty-second birthday, his new forty-three-year-old manager said, "Well, now that you are sixty-two [early retirement age under the company's pension plan] and fully vested [his pension benefits were guaranteed] under the pension plan, I guess you'll be retiring." When Andy told him he was *not*, he was hit with a flurry of critical memos (designed to "build a case" against Andy) accusing him of all sorts of performance deficiencies, whereas he had never in the past received even a single memo, critical or otherwise. In the ensuing months, Andy's boss became increasingly aggressive in his unwarranted criticism and eventually fired him.

Looking at the timing (Andy's sixty-second birthday) of the change in attitude by Andy's boss (which triggered the onslaught of manufactured criticism), Andy and I decided to file suit on his behalf. The state agency complaint was filed and subsequently withdrawn, and then suit was filed in federal court. Eventually, the discovery process was completed and a date was picked to select a jury for trial. Then, about a week before jury selection, the attorney for the insurance company notified the court he had just discovered that Andy had agreed to arbitrate any dispute he had with the company, and the insurance company made a motion to compel arbitration.

Arbitration is a more informal procedure, agreed to by the parties, in which one or more neutral persons called arbitrators are selected by the parties to resolve any controversies that arise between them. Although the proceedings before the arbitrators are not governed by the same strict rules of evidence that apply in court, arbitration awards (decisions) are just as binding and even less likely to be reversed on appeal.

Proponents of arbitration like this process because it is

a faster, less-expensive way of adjudicating legal disputes. Opponents dislike the idea that the arbitration proceedings are not governed by the same rules of evidence that apply to court proceedings nor are the arbitrators obligated to abide by any laws in reaching their decision—they can do so . . . but they need not.

While I recognize that arbitration may be suitable for some persons, I don't like it, particularly as a means of resolving employment discrimination claims. On a broad level, I am not comfortable with a process in which there is no jury and there are no procedural rules to follow or laws to be complied with. Nor do I like the fact that the arbitrators (usually selected jointly by the parties from an available pool) are not required to have any knowledge or expertise in the area of employment discrimination, especially when errors on their part are not grounds for appeal. The very limited basis for appealing an adverse arbitration award is that the arbitrators acted in an "arbitrary and capricious" manner. As I said, making mistakes of law or fact does not qualify as "arbitrary and capricious." To overturn an arbitration award, it is usually necessary to show that the award bears no relation to the evidence or that the arbitrators acted in an unethical or irrational manner.

Basically, in exchange for speed and informality in processing a case, arbitration offers "substantial justice." Well, "substantial" (meaning "in large measure") is not good enough for me. For my clients, I want to get as close to *real* justice as possible.

In Andy's case, it seems that when he joined the insurance company, he was required to obtain a license to sell securities as part of the estate planning aspect of his duties. Buried in the license application in small print was the agreement to submit all disputes to arbitration. In truth, Andy hadn't read it and was totally unaware of its existence. The insurance company, which should have known of its existence because all its salesmen are required to apply for the license, claimed it had lost sight of it because Andy was now in management.

For many years, those in the legal profession who shared my point of view took the position that arbitration agreements, such as that in Andy's license application, did not cover claims of employment discrimination. Unfortunately, in 1991, the Supreme Court ruled that they did. Nonetheless, I saw no advantage to pursuing arbitration at that point, as the case was scheduled to go to a jury in a matter of days, and I told this to the court.

The judge, however, felt he had no choice (a conclusion with which I disagreed) but to send the case to arbitration because of court policy favoring arbitration as a quick and efficient way of resolving disputes *and* lightening the caseload of the courts. In so doing, the judge did manifest his displeasure with the insurance company by imposing sanctions (penalties) against it, directing the insurance company to pay $2,000 to my client. Considering the loss of the chance to have a jury decide his case, this was little consolation.

I would like to have appealed this decision immediately, but because of a quirk in the law that makes a denial of the request for arbitration appealable, but not an order compelling arbitration, I was prevented from doing so until the end of the lawsuit. By then, of course, it would serve little purpose.

Then, to make matters worse, the organization that schedules and conducts the arbitrations, the National Association of Securities Dealers (NASD), was backlogged. Despite my requests, it refused to expedite Andy's case. Weeks turned into months, and when Andy's case had still not been scheduled for almost a year, in frustration, I sought the help of the judge who had sent the case to arbitration. This time he didn't fail us. He told us (myself and counsel for the insurance company) that he was ready to drag the NASD into court and order them to schedule Andy's case at once. When I told the NASD representative of the judge's intention, we had our hearing two weeks later before a panel of three arbitrators.

But the horror story was not over. During the four days of hearings, my worst fears about arbitrators were confirmed. According to the NASD's rules, one member of the panel had to be an "industry" arbitrator. This means he is the representative (and usually an employee) of the securities or insurance industry. The name "industry arbitrator" says it all. What employee or his attorney could be comfortable seeking a favorable decision from the "industry's" representative? Certainly not me.

Our second arbitrator had a Ph.D. in some unrelated discipline and distinguished himself by asking questions that made it obvious he hadn't been listening to the testimony. For example, he questioned a number of witnesses about their attitudes toward fellow employees of the opposite sex, apparently having lost sight of the fact that this was an age discrimination, not a sex discrimination, case.

Worst of all, however, was the chairperson of the panel, who was herself an attorney. It was painful to see her go out of her way to assist the insurance company's witnesses. She repeatedly intruded herself into my cross-examination to make such solicitous remarks as "Did you really understand the question?" and "You look confused, do you need that question rephrased?" and "You seem uncomfortable, do you need a break?" Needless to say, I forcefully voiced my objections to these improper interruptions, but with little success. Of course, the witnesses were uncomfortable. I was putting them in the position where it was becoming clear to all concerned that they were not testifying truthfully.

In any event, when the hearings concluded, I had a bad feeling about the outcome. And I was right! A couple of months later, after several unexplained delays, we received a one-page decision in favor of the insurance company. There was no explanation of the basis for the arbitrators' award. Andy took the loss philosophically (probably better than I), has a new job, and is saving for his retirement.

It made no sense to appeal the decision, given the very limited basis for having it overturned. However, because Andy's case had now concluded, we were finally able to appeal the court's order that sent it to arbitration in the first place. If the Court of Appeals agrees that the insurance company's motion to compel arbitration came too late in the process, Andy will get a new trial before a jury rather than a panel of arbitrators.

What this all shows is that it is dangerous to put the fox in charge of the henhouse. How long would the securities and insurance industries require their employees to submit their disputes to arbitration at the NASD if that organization consistently issued decisions in favor of the employee? And how often would individuals acting as arbitrators (who obviously like the power and fees conferred on them) be selected from the list of potential arbitrators if their decisions were consistently adverse to the "industry"? There surely are those who believe that the vested interest of the organization and its arbitrators in keeping the "industry" happy taints the process.

The moral: Read the small print—in an employment— or any—contract!

Chapter 13

The Pros and Cons of Settlement

A funny thing happens on the way to the forum—in this case, the court. About eight out of ten cases headed in that direction never get there because they are settled.

Settlement (the end result of a negotiating process between the attorneys) generally is an agreement between the parties whereby the employer pays its employee, or more likely its former employee, a sum of money—usually *more* than it would like to pay, but *less* than it could lose at trial. For his or her part, the employee accepts a sum that is *less* than could be awarded by the jury, but *more* than the zero he or she would receive if the jury ruled in favor of the employer. Settlement is a compromise that eliminates risk.

For all the reasons discussed throughout this book, when the moment of truth approaches, many employers would rather run than take a hit. And many plaintiffs opt for a bird in the hand, rather than risk losing at trial.

How does this work? At some point during the progress of your case, the possibility of settlement will probably be raised by one of the lawyers. Should this not occur, the judge assigned to the case may make a *strong* suggestion to that end. The motive of the lawyers is obvious—sidestep the risk that the case could go entirely against their client.

As for the judge, the court system itself has a vested interest in this seemingly beneficent suggestion—every case that's settled means one less case on the judge's overloaded calendar.

There is even a section in the federal court procedural rules specifically designed to foster the voluntary resolution of lawsuits. It provides that if the defendant (employer) offers to allow the plaintiff (employee) to enter judgment (a court order) against it for a specific amount, and the offer is rejected by the plaintiff, and the jury subsequently awards the plaintiff a sum that is less than that offered by the defendant, the plaintiff will not be entitled to recover costs or attorney's fees incurred after the date of the offer.

At first blush, this looks like something employers who are being sued for employment discrimination should take advantage of. This rule will, particularly if used early in the litigation process, put pressure on the employee. Obviously, the higher the offer, the greater the pressure. But even a lowball throwaway offer would seem to have some advantage to the employer. Even if it is rejected by the worker, it could mean a great deal, depending on the size of the jury verdict.

So why is this option rarely utilized? Two principal reasons: First, the employer, particularly early in the game, is still optimistic that it will prevail at trial, or alternatively, that it can overwhelm the employee and run him out of the game. Second, and perhaps the more pervasive reason, is that the procedure involves more than settlement. As the name "entry of judgment" indicates, there will be an *actual court judgment on file* against the employer. Unlike true settlement agreements, which generally provide that their terms are confidential, a judgment means that the employer has been found *guilty* of the infractions charged and the terms of the judgment are available for public scrutiny.

The *timing* of settlement discussions is very important. Are they taking place early in the game or closer to trial? Is it before or after a motion for summary judgment has been made? The answers to these questions will reveal a great deal about which party may be feeling more vulnerable emotionally or financially. For example, in the initial stages of litigation, the employee may still be nervous and leery about the legal process (and the myths and misconceptions that surround it) and more willing to settle "just to be done with it." Conversely, the employer may well be angry at the temerity of his ex-employee to sue him, and disdainful of the employee's prospects. In my experience, this is the time at which the employer can probably get the best deal, but also in my experience, it rarely happens because employers don't pursue it.

At the other end of the spectrum, eve of trial, the employee has essentially absorbed, withstood, and survived the best the company has to offer in terms of financial and psychological intimidation. The worker's confidence is buoyed, and he or she is looking forward to their day in court, for the opportunity to confront the former employer as equals in the eyes of what is probably viewed as a sympathetic jury. The great risk here for the employer is that the employee may want that day in court so badly that he or she will not be receptive to even a reasonable offer of settlement. Eve-of-trial settlements are probably *the most expensive* for the employer, and the most commonplace.

To be sure, at either of these polar ends of settlement negotiations, the lawyers should play a positive role. They can do their clients a great service by getting them to rise above emotions and look at the real advantages and disadvantages of settling.

In my opinion, the best opportunity for settlement is after discovery has been completed, when emotions are on the back burner and each party has a true appreciation for the pros and cons of his and the other side's case. If the parties do not seize this opportunity, and the employer decides to move for summary judgment, the roller coaster will be off and running again. The motion will certainly place the employee at risk, but denial of the motion by the court will pump up the employee's optimism for success at trial. Neither of these situations creates an atmosphere conducive to settlement.

At best, settlement negotiations are an imprecise science, depending as they do on competing views of the likelihood that either party will prevail at trial. However, once under way, the process is predictable. If the company's lawyers make the first offer, it will usually be low ball, meaning the employer will offer less than it thinks will be accepted. On the other hand, if your lawyer starts the ball rolling, it will be with a high-ball (inflated) demand. Then, after more consultations with their respective clients (the company on the one hand, and you on the other), the lawyers will negotiate and try to come up with an amount, usually somewhere in the middle, that both parties can live with.

While our discussion has focused on financial settlements, because these are most common, the possibility of other arrangements should not be overlooked—for example, the offer by the company to grant the promotion that had been denied, or to reemploy the worker who had been fired, in exchange for withdrawal of the discrimination claim.

I was actually quite surprised not long ago when, shortly after filing an age discrimination suit, my client's former employer, a large luggage manufacturer, offered, as a means of settling the lawsuit, to reemploy her in a job similar to the one she had held prior to her discharge. This was feasible because my client had been terminated in a downsizing that, according to the company, resulted in the elimination of her job. It was not a case in which she had been accused of poor performance or misconduct, so there was not the same type of acrimony involved. Our case had not challenged the legitimacy of the downsizing but rather the company's failure to make as diligent an effort to find a new position for this fifty-four-year-old woman as it had for younger employees whose jobs had also been eliminated. When the company also agreed to pay my legal fee (so that my client was not made to suffer any out-of-pocket costs in getting her job back), the case was settled.

Remember, ultimately, the decision whether to accept any settlement offer will be up to you. Your lawyer will help, but in evaluating your options, there are questions you should ask yourself (keeping in mind that the employer will likely be going through a similar questioning process):

1. *How strong are your own beliefs about the merits of your case?* You have to be as objective as possible about this because, in the end, no matter what discovery has revealed, no matter how weak your employer's defenses may seem to be, the outcome of any trial is always in doubt. There are no guarantees. The best you

can do is try to have a reasonable opinion as to the strengths and weaknesses of your case.

2. *How positive does your attorney feel about a jury trial?* You've paid for his advice; listen carefully to what he or she has to say. He is an expert who makes this evaluation all the time, whereas for you it is probably a one-time experience. If your attorney feels strongly one way or the other, you should give his opinion serious consideration. But don't simply accept his conclusion. Ask him to explain his reasons.

3. *How large a settlement has been offered?* The first calculation to make is a comparison of the offer made by the company to the amount you could win at trial. I've told you about the possibilities for front pay, back pay, damages for emotional distress, punitive damages, and the rest. You should know by now—but if not, ask your lawyer, immediately, for his *conservative* opinion as to what you might be awarded by a jury. Obviously, the higher the company's offer, the more difficult it is to reject it. While there is no exact formula, one rule of thumb is to give great consideration to a settlement offer that is half or more of what you *might* receive at trial.

4. *How are you handling the financial costs of the lawsuit?* If you are on a contingency fee arrangement or have a minimum fee/contingency fee arrangement, this may not be a crucial inquiry because you have already reached the limit of your financial obligations. If not, and you are being billed by the hour, it most certainly will be. As it turns out, this question may be

of more concern to the employer. Remember the case we discussed earlier involving the huge conglomerate whose management had sexually harassed, demoted, and then discharged my client? As I told you, the rapidly escalating costs of defending that case played no small part in the company's initiating settlement discussions.

5.   *Are you a gambler? A person who is comfortable taking risks?* Or, are you a believer in the maxim that a bird in the hand is worth two in the bush? Because that's really what it comes down to. Here's a settlement case history of one client who decided to "roll the dice": This sixty-year-old, who had been earning $50,000 a year, was terminated and then sued her former company on the basis of age discrimination. If the case were to go to trial within a year and a half, the jury could award about $950,000 (based on doubled back pay and benefits of $150,000, front pay of $750,000, and perhaps $50,000 for emotional distress, plus my legal fees of about $100,000). The judge had urged the lawyers to discuss a settlement. After negotiating, the best offer was $250,000. My client said: "If we don't get $500,000, let's go to trial." She had asked herself all the questions posed above, but she felt that being put out to pasture prematurely, coupled with having had no luck finding another job, required her to "go for it." The trial is pending—we'll see whether she made the right decision.

I have had other clients, who, when faced with similar numbers and possibilities, opted for that bird in the hand.

There really is no right or wrong choice. It's a personal decision that depends on the individual personality and the unique circumstances of each case. Just think it through carefully and be prepared to live with the decision, whatever it may be. There will be no benefit in second-guessing yourself later on.

Afterword

I hope that no matter what else you take away with you from reading this book, you will understand that no one, neither lawyers nor anyone else, can put themselves in your shoes or know what you went through or how you feel about your experience. (If it's any help, one of my clients, knowing I was writing this book, offered to make *her personal experiences* available, and they appear in the Appendix.)

This book is, in no small measure, about *choice*. Almost nobody wants to get involved in lawsuits and, *given a choice,* would not do so. But when employment discrimination costs you your job, or a promotion, or anything else, and you pay the price financially and in loss of self-esteem, and everything else that goes along with it, *not* suing may no longer be a viable *choice*. Wishing that it hadn't happened to you won't be enough. The *choice* is now to make the best of two options, neither of which you would have chosen had *you* been given a *choice* by your employer.

If, deep in your heart, you believe you suffered employment discrimination, then seek professional advice, talk to your family and friends, do some research, carefully consider your options, and make a studied and sensible decision about what you want to do and how you want to proceed. For any number of reasons, it may make sense for you to forget the whole experience, put it behind you, and get on with your life. But if everything tells you to pursue what you believe is a just cause, the right cause, with an employment discrimination suit, don't be deterred by things that don't count.

With tenacity, and good fortune, and a good lawyer, my guess is that most of you will do quite well.

Appendix: Getting There (to Trial) Is Not Half the Fun

Jo's Story

That April day in 1994 had started out beautifully. I was wearing a new bright blue straw hat—my colleagues at the major publishing company where I worked as publicity director called me the "Hat Lady"—and at my first meeting of the day, my boss admired my hat *and* the press release I had worked on until 12:30 A.M. the night before. She said: "Jo, you're wonderful."

Six hours later she asked me to *resign!* I really was stunned. For over three years I had gotten steady raises, bonuses, and accolades. The reasons for this "termination," she said, were that I spent too much company time on personal business (I had had an intern photocopy my financial papers because I was trying to refinance my house) and that the "morale" in my department was "bad." I refuted these points: She and everyone else at the company knew I worked nights and weekends, using *personal time* for *company business;* as for morale, my current assistant was stumbling badly (and I had asked her to look for a job more suited to her temperament), and my former assistant, whom I had promoted to publicity manager, would have liked *my* job. I asked for a chance to discuss the situation;

she said, "This is definite—there's no discussion. Hand in your keys to personnel." I said, "No way will I resign—you will have to fire me." And she did.

As I drove home that afternoon, fortunately without killing myself or anyone else, I realized my sixtieth birthday was just three months away, and for the first time in my life, I felt *old!* In fact, I became a senior citizen in *just twenty-seven minutes*—the time it took for them to fire me, and for me to pack up my personal belongings.

My three grown-up kids raised the specter of "age discrimination." Although I looked young, acted young, felt young, and like Jack Benny, only admitted to being thirty-nine, and always described myself, in the genteel French way, as "a woman of a certain age," I couldn't deny the facts, or even the relevance of fiction. I had been caught in an *All About Eve* situation, where I set myself up for the fall. Although I'm no Bette Davis, my former assistant, Claudia, could have outplayed Ann Baxter as Eve. Age? Why else had I been fired? I had just gotten a raise and bonus a few months earlier. That realization caused me to look through my files—I'm a pack rat who saves everything—until I found a magazine article about age bias.

And that's how I found Mr. Bernbach. Of course, after all this time, we are on "Jeff" and "Jo" terms because we "work" so closely together. When we first talked I was scared, upset, really shocked, and not surprisingly, *angry,* that my company could do this to me. Jeff calmed me down and said he thought I had a viable case. The first thing he warned me was: "Don't sign any releases/waivers when you get your severance pay, because that would eliminate your right to sue." So, I didn't.

Next, he filed the appropriate papers for me with the EEOC, and they subsequently sent on the Right to Sue notice. Then we filed a lawsuit in federal court and the papers about the suit had to be served on my company. That was painless to me, after all I didn't have to present the subpoenas personally. But I did take some pleasure in knowing that now they *knew* I wasn't going to go gently into that dark night, to borrow from Dylan Thomas. A few quiet months went by while this was happening; my severance pay hadn't run out yet, so I had this "false" notion of still receiving a weekly paycheck. I was also getting my unemployment and looking for job opportunities, so nothing had impacted on me financially, *yet*. I guess you could call this the "calm before the storm." But I felt rudderless, restless. I had *loved* my job, and I felt bad about "abandoning" the authors I had worked so hard for.

By the fall of 1994, we began the discovery process. The first step was answering what are called "interrogatories," where the lawyers for my former company wanted all kinds of information: my tax returns for the last five years, my medical records for *ten* years, my résumé and employment record for *my entire life,* my records of job searches. *Everything*. At the same time, Jeff sent "interrogatories" to the people at my ex-company who were involved in my firing, asking them to corroborate their reasons for firing me.

Months went by, my unemployment ran out. I was borrowing money from my *kids*. Now, instead of me taking care of them, they were worrying about taking care of *me*. I had no job offers, and for the first time in my life, my blood pressure was way too high. It had always been a steady 120 over 80; now it was 160 over 90, and varied, sometimes up to 195 over 95. When you lose your job, from out of nowhere suddenly you develop antennae about similar things, and I began to realize just how strong emotional distress can be. (Actually, this was not so different from what had happened to me when my husband died in 1974, and I knew from reading about stress tests that after the death of a mate, and divorce, the loss of a job is *third* on the stress barometer.) Being terminated (or getting terminated, I don't know which is correct) really screws you up emotionally and financially.

I remember saving one article headlined "Getting Laid Off Can Lay You Up," which said that a stretch of unemployment weakens your immune system and can cause other illnesses because unemployment is depressing. Well, I really didn't have to read that to know it. I began to have recurring headaches. Were they caused by tension? High blood pressure? Or both. I had resolved to stop smoking and I failed—*miserably*. I didn't sleep well, and when I did I had anxiety-ridden dreams: My house was burning, something was happening to my children, my teeth were falling out.

The day of deposition finally arrived. My deposition and *their* depositions had been postponed and postponed for months, which doesn't add to one's composure. You gear yourself up for the appointment, and it . . . doesn't happen. Then you have to go through the self-bolstering all over again. This may sound dumb, but I anguished over what to wear. Should I look old? Should I look young? Should I wear my best business clothes? Should I show up in jeans? The final choice was something in the middle. I was *scared*. Nobody likes confrontations. And I was confronted by two, count them, *two* big corporate-type lawyers representing the publisher. Jeff, of course, was right there with me, and only kicked me in the ankle twice. I tend to talk too much, I guess because of my career as a PR person. When you give a deposition, you're only supposed to answer the *exact* question put to you, and not go into other details.

(Later I felt like an expert when watching the O. J. Simpson trial. "Just answer yes or no," I would yell at the TV screen.) Those industrial-grade lawyers for my former employer, clearly on a fishing expedition, asked me questions going back *thirty-plus years* about my work history, my partners, the people who had worked for me, my marriages, my lifestyle, my kids, my relations with co-workers. The session lasted six hours with a one-hour break for lunch.

To put it mildly, this is a very difficult experience to go through. Most of us aren't used to being "grilled" by two high-powered attorneys, taking notes on *everything* you say. After a while I started to get the rhythm, and the lawyers became less intimidating. At first, I felt I hadn't really gotten across the fact that I had been discriminated against because of my age. I thought, in a way, that I had let Jeff down. But he pointed out to me in our "postgame wrap-up" that I had done okay, and that our opportunity to establish the age bias would come when *they* gave their depositions.

A couple of days later, their depositions began. I don't know how other lawyers do it, but Jeff wanted me there for all five depositions. I would be in the presence of Claudia (the Eve in the story), the president of the publishing conglomerate, the publisher of my division, the human resources director, and last, but not least, my immediate boss,

Jennifer, the marketing V.P. Jeff warned me not to get upset because I would probably be hearing lies about me. I said, "They're under oath." He said, "They may still lie."

And they did. When I walked into the room, Jennifer said, "Hi, Jo," in a hearty way, with a big smile, as if I were some long-lost friend. I almost responded in kind until I realized that this was my *enemy*, she had been the *executioner* who had *fired* me. Jennifer's deposition was very chilling. She didn't exactly lie, but she didn't tell the truth either. And aside from that first warm greeting, which I aborted, she spent six or seven uncomfortable hours *not* making eye contact with me. Her composure began to crumble. Jennifer had provided notes, as part of the "interrogatories," of my attendance records, which she said were made daily, but they were written in backward fashion; in other words, latest dates first. Who keeps a diary that way? Jeff called her on this. "Didn't you prepare these notes after the fact, just for this case?" he asked. She answered no, but her darting eyes gave her away. She also had a listing of the times I had been out for snow during that horrendous winter of 1994. Jeff pointed out that there had been seventeen separate snowstorms amounting to fifty-six inches of snow . . . and that although I hadn't come into the office on some of those days, my phone records indicated that I had been working on the company's behalf at home. In the end, Jennifer could not really explain *why* I had been fired. (In the postmortem, Jeff told me he thought we had established some very positive points.)

The deposition of the publisher was next and was also unnerving. He said he had met with me only *two or three times* over the course of three years (the number was really closer to *forty or fifty*, and I still cherish the notes on which he wrote, "Good job, Jo!"). Although he said he would never fire anyone for photocopying personal papers, he also couldn't quite explain *why* I had been fired, and really seemed to be out of the entire loop of my termination. Jeff thought the publisher had inadvertently helped our case.

Third at bat was the human resources director, who was pretty straightforward. All she really did was confirm that I had worked there, had gotten raises and bonuses, and had never received any warnings for performance. Jeff told me the last point was important because since the "official" reason given for my discharge was "performance," there was no record of any warnings regarding my performance.

But the interviews with Claudia and the president of the publishing conglomerate really floored me, and at the same time made me feel optimistic about my case. Claudia came into the meeting looking very sure of herself, but not looking at me, of course. She told Jeff she had been doing most of my job because I spent *hours* every day on personal matters. So Jeff asked her about the office and phone setup and said, "How did you know how much time Mrs. Bennett [me] was spending on personal details? And how did you spend *hours* doing her work if you were spending hours observing her conduct her personal business? And who did *your* job if you were doing hers?" She got more than a little flustered trying to explain this. I am not a vindictive person, but I confess that I began to feel good about Claudia's obvious discomfort. (I found out later that both Jennifer and Claudia, during breaks in their depositions, had told Jeff's secretary how *distraught* and *destroyed* they felt about Jeff's questioning.)

To help prepare for the depositions it was *very* important for me to scrape my brain and remember anything that could be relevant to my case. This was an example: Claudia denied any personal interest I had taken in her over the course of three years. Jeff, however, armed with his own sharp awareness of the scene, and some issues I had come up with for him, made Ms. Claudia very uncomfortable. He produced color photos of times she had been to my home and my summerhouse, photos showing her with her arm around me. He also asked her about gifts I had given, and times I had taken care of her at my home when she was ill. And then he said to the girl I had treated like a daughter, "So you stabbed Jo in the back!"

Claudia had also testified that she felt she could do my job, even though she had only had a little more than two years' experience, and implied that maybe I wasn't as up on computer technology as she was. But Jeff didn't let her get away with this and actually made her acknowledge that I had taught her everything she knew about publicity. He also got her to admit that she was looking for another job because she didn't want to work under my direction. In other words, she wanted to be *the boss*.

But maybe the most astounding testimony was that of the president of the parent company. His deposition actually filled in the parts of the puzzle that had been missing. He admitted that he had talked to Claudia, heard her complaints about me, and ultimately had given in to her "either her or me" demand, without ever talking to *me*. Mr. Smith, let's call him, who is an attorney, and as Jeff pointed out, should have known better, chose a subordinate's word over mine, without even affording me a chance to tell my side. This was a serious error. In fact, he, the head of this conglomerate, had *descended* to our floor to meet with Claudia. (Jeff picked up on this and asked him "Why?") It also turned out that Mr. Smith, together with Mr. Brown, a "bean counter," as Jeff calls him, had been two of the three corporate biggies who had decided to approve Claudia's "either/or" proposal. Mr. Brown always liked Claudia's hair and was known to fondle it on elevator rides. (Claudia did not like this and thought such gestures were "politically incorrect," but never did anything about protesting.)

At the conclusion of Mr. Smith's testimony, I began to feel much better about my case. Nonetheless, all of this had tremendous personal impact on me. Of course I felt better that my chances of being vindicated seemed to improve because of the *statements* made during these depositions, and the *admissions* that Jeff was able to establish. ("Mr. Smith, you, a member of the New York bar, never gave Mrs. Bennett, a *senior executive* of your company, an opportunity to present her side of the case?????") Still, your emotions can't be shelved. You go about your job, think you're providing the right stuff for your company, get all the praises and raises, and then find out that the megaboss decides to fire you on the word of a pretty young thing half your age. That hurts.

And all during these depositions, everyone looked out the window, instead of making eye contact (although Jeff had advised me to look them right in the eye). I found myself looking out the window occasionally, too, to see what was so interesting out there. Another weird thing about the depositions was that during the formal testimony, their lawyers and my lawyer were very gruff with each other—'OBJECT' and all that stuff—but during the breaks they were so cordial and friendly. (Again, that's the way it was during the O. J. trial: The lawyers, all eighty or whatever, were so adversarial, and then during breaks they exchanged jokes.)

Jeff had told me that during these depositions I should pass him notes if anything occurred to me that might be helpful, and I did. *Dozens of notes.* Later I realized I was scribbling these missives on obsolete JO BENNETT, PUBLICITY DIRECTOR memo pads from my job. That was sad for me. Maybe in part of my mind I still thought of myself as the "publicity director." But the notes help you get through a helpless feeling. After all, you are hearing all these nasty untruths about yourself, and you can't get up and strangle the person or yell "liar."

However, the depositions did not nearly begin to represent closure. Next came what John Housman so dramatically described in the famous TV attorney series, the "Paper Chase." The company's lawyers threatened to bring a summary judgment motion, which as we all know by now represents the greatest vulnerability to a plaintiff because it asks the judge to throw out the lawsuit without even going to trial.

I had a brief crisis of confidence over this, of course, which was swiftly countered by Jeff's big-muscle threat of sanctions against *them* for their frivolous actions. The motions flew back and forth; their lawyers backed off on summary judgment, and I then spent the next months working closely with Jeff, thwarting still more bizarre attempts to prove what a wretched employee I had been.

Of course the reinstatement of my professional reputation, via a victory in what seems like a forever case, is yet to come in what has actually taken less than two years from that spring day I was terminated. Right now, I've rejected what I felt was an inadequate offer for settlement, and we

are waiting for the trial to be scheduled. But a very important, positive take on all of this is that I was really *partici-
pating* in my case. I wasn't just sitting back and letting it
all happen to me. I think that's crucial, because when you
lose your job, in many ways you feel so acted upon, so *pas-
sive*. Something has been done to you over which you had
no control. But if you work with a lawyer you can relate
to, you will be able to have an *active* role in your case and
be able to feel you are doing something to help yourself.
This is really significant, no matter how the case turns out.

Index

ABOUT THE AUTHOR

Jeffrey M. Bernbach is a New York City attorney specializing in employment discrimination cases. In more than twenty-five years of practice, he has successfully represented hundreds of clients, ranging from individuals to Fortune 500 companies, in job bias lawsuits.

Mr. Bernbach spent several years practicing with the prestigious Wall Street law firm Cravath, Swaine & Moore, until leaving to assume the position of Chief Labor Counsel with The Hearst Corporation. For the past eighteen years he has been in his own law practice.

Mr. Bernbach has also served as legal advisor to a Member of the National Labor Relations Board in Washington, D.C., a Member of the New York State Governor's Advisory Council on Employment and Unemployment Insurance, and is presently a Member and Chairman of the Audit and Finance Committee of the New York State Job Development Authority.